MANAGING CHILDREN'S BEHAVIOUR

A PRACTICAL GUIDE FOR NURSERY PROFESSIONALS

RUTH ANDRESKI AND SARAH NICHOLLS

NURSERY WORLD

A NURSERY WORLD BOOK

Second Edition

NURSERY WORLD

A NURSERY WORLD BOOK

Second Edition

Second edition published in Great Britain by
Times Supplements Limited
Admiral House, 66–68 East Smithfield
London E1 9XY

2 4 6 8 10 9 7 5 3 1

A CIP catalogue record for this book is available from the British Library

ISBN 1-84122-001-9

Printed and bound in Belgium

First published in 1997 by Nursery World Limited

ISBN 1-899514-02-3

Photography: Andy Crawford
Additional photography: Arran Media Resources

CONTENTS

INTRODUCTION

This book is written mainly for early years professionals in care and education settings. Interested parents may also find it useful when judging such settings or in their dealings with their own children. We use the term nursery to include all pre-school establishments. It is not a book about 'crisis scenarios', where everybody is at their wits' ends, although we have devoted one chapter to such situations. We have chosen to take a broad view in relation to managing children's behaviour and believe in the old adage that prevention is better than cure. To this end we have spent some time looking at possible underlying causes for troublesome behaviour. Without an understanding of the causes it is difficult, if not impossible, to rectify, or at least improve troublesome behaviour.

The very long period of infant and childhood dependency necessitates a good deal of self sacrifice and altruism on the part of carers. This, and the fact that humans need to co-operate in almost all they do, demonstrates that elements of 'goodness' are very much part of our innate character. Unfortunately, we also have the propensity to be selfish and are capable of all kinds of nasty things in order to satisfy our appetites and desires. Our success as educators in helping to get the balance right is of crucial importance, not just for society, but also for individual happiness.

Psychology has taught us how the treatment of the very young influences, to a large extent, their view of themselves and their attitudes to others. In writing this book we have drawn not only on our knowledge of current theory, but above all, on our own experiences after lifelong work in the education of young children. Our case study materials are born out of this experience. We give particular attention to the crucial role of parents in developing children's emotional well-being – chapter six is devoted to the parents' role.

We have also considered the importance of the adult's role in interacting with children, creating the right environment and planning those parts of the curriculum which are primarily concerned with the expression of feelings and the development of a sense of responsibility. In addition, we know that many settings use television and video and that all settings use literature as part of their educational programme. We have suggested ways of using these media to their full potential to influence positive attitudes and behaviour.

We recognise children's need for a consistent framework for discipline, and to this end present a Behaviour Policy for discussion and consideration by professional groups and parents. This policy focuses upon positive rather than negative rules.

For ease of reading we use the male form when writing in the second person. Where we use he/him and so on, she/her and so on applies equally. Finally, we hope readers will find the book free of unnecessary jargon and that it will help them, in a practical way, to tackle this area of major concern.

1: THE NATIONAL PICTURE

EVERY TIME A NEW AND SHOCKING REVELATION about children's behaviour hits the headlines, both politicians and public thrash about to find explanations and answers. There are no shortage of scapegoats identified by the great and the good among us, who pontificate from their safe and often distant positions. In the meantime, experienced practitioners working with young children and their families feel a certain sense of unease. It has become increasingly obvious to them that the way our society brings up its children is failing for a variety of reasons. They have observed, at first hand, a change for the worse in children's behaviour. Indeed an overwhelming number of respondents to our questionnaire in *Nursery World* magazine[1] agreed that behaviour had deteriorated over the past ten years.

Moreover, professionals in childcare and education find that increasing demands are made on them to such an extent that they can be asked to try to compensate for poor parenting and, at worst, repair damage caused by neglect or abuse. We will discuss in this chapter some of the factors we think are responsible for this state of affairs.

THE CHANGING NATURE OF FAMILY AND COMMUNITY

To say that there ever was a 'golden age' for family life is probably unrealistic. There has, however, been a very clear shift from the time when a family almost invariably consisted of two parents and their children, supported by a network of relatives and neighbours of long standing – what sociologists call the

[1] R. Andreski, S. Nicholls 'Who's In Control in Your Nursery?'
Nursery World (22 August 1996)

extended family. Communities were much more stable in the past, people tended to work close to home and were less mobile, and the breadwinner often did the same job for a lifetime. Change occurred much more slowly, and a certain sense of security could be gained from the orderliness in a community where everyone knew everyone else and roles and relationships, customs and beliefs were more clearly defined and more universally shared.

Sebastian's picture of his friend Jenny.

Julianne's picture of her friend Martha.

Hannahs picture of her Auntie.

Today, we live in a time of rapid social change brought about in large measure by the information technology revolution. The nature of work has altered for many people and there is greater insecurity. This has been a major factor in breaking up the extended family into nuclear units, often living at some distance from each other and therefore unable to offer the example and support available in former times. These changes have put pressure on families. Parents who find that marriage does not live up to their expectations seek a way out through divorce, so that now nearly one quarter of families with dependent children have only one parent – in 90% of cases this is the mother. Such changes have clearly been hard on children because not only do they suffer the 'loss' of a parent, their financial situation deteriorates, too, and the remaining parent bears the pressure of doing the work of two people. A staggering 2.3 million children in this country now live with a single parent in this situation[2].

[2] Andreas Whittam Smith 'A Government Policy Stolen From King Canute' *The Independent* (2 December 1996)

If the separation of parents is acrimonious, the children suffer even more by acting as pawns in a particularly nasty game. When this happens the father – for it is almost always the father – is frequently absent from the scene. When the father leaves the family home his relatives – including the granparents, uncles, aunts and cousins – will probably stop seeing the children so regularly, too. Another worrying feature of this situation is that when parents remarry, children are required to make difficult emotional adjustments to a new web of relationships. Today, one in twelve children live in step families.

THE CHANGING SITUATION FOR MEN AND WOMEN AT WORK

Generally speaking, women today are better educated and have much higher career expectations than their predecessors. Seeking success in their own right is no doubt in part due to their perception of the insecurity of marriage as a career and the cult of individuality which has characterised the past twenty years or so. Moreover, as technology has advanced more jobs have become available to women. Approximately two thirds of mothers now work, albeit some part time. The dual role of motherhood and career is demanding, particularly in high-powered jobs. Inevitably there must be less time for children and certainly a lot less of that unhurried time to listen and share experiences. Perhaps this has played a part in the increase in referrals of children to child guidance clinics. Indeed, as a recent research study conducted by the West Berkshire Health Authority and Reading University's Psychology Department has shown, problems with young children are spread right across the social spectrum[3].

It would be unfair, however, just to blame the absence of Mum from the scene. Today's father is required to work such long hours, often even sacrificing weekends, that he can almost become a stranger in his own home. The cult of the workaholic may seem to make sense to the business community, but we disagree. Short-term gain may appear advantageous to a company, but the long term consequences of employing stressed

[3] Dr Arlene Vetere et al., Reading University, article on research published September 1996, *The Independent* (25 August 1996)

and burnt-out parents will be grave. After all, tomorrow's workforce depends upon the children of today growing into well adjusted adults. Secure emotional bonding between children and parents can only be achieved by children and parents spending quality time together, and a recent Mintel survey revealed 20% of parents admitting to NO PLEASURE from time with their children[4].

CHANGES IN PARENTAL ATTITUDES TO CHILDREN'S FREEDOM

Today's parents are very apprehensive about letting their children out on their own, even though the statistics show that there are no more child murders and abductions now than there were 25 years ago when 80% of seven- and eight-year-olds walked to school unaccompanied by an adult. By 1990 only 9% were doing so. In a recent survey nearly half the parents questioned said they never, or hardly ever, let their children play out without adult supervision. This caution is as much to do with the density of traffic, with its inherent dangers, as it is with the fear of madmen (or women)[5].

The negative result of this fear is, of course, that many challenges and opportunities, such as pitting their wits against the forces of nature, problem solving and sorting out relationships for themselves, are denied to children. Because few adults are willing to accompany children out of doors for as long as they would like, or need, the result is often confinement.

Confinement leads to lack of exercise and reduction of physical development, which in turn has a number of undesirable consequences for children. Children are unlikely to be able to develop bodily functions such as circulation and respiration to their full capacity resulting in important negative consequences for their health in later life.

Confinement is also likely to build up a kind of frustration that can only be released through vigorous physical activity, popularly known as 'letting off steam'. We wonder how many so-

[4] Mintel Survey, 'Give Children Time Not Television' *Sunday Times* (2 June 1996)

[5] Barry Hugill, 'The Horror of Being a Child In the Nineties: Findings from Policy Studies Institute Think Tank Study' *The Observer* (8 August 1993)

called hyperactive individuals are really only very energetic children who need to run about outside until they are tired!

And it is not just children's physical development that is likely to be impaired through keeping them indoors too much. According to a recent newspaper article, Dr Ned Mueller, a clinical psychologist, claims that confinement can retard intellectual development as well! In another article, Dr Elizabeth Newsome of Nottingham University says that children are not learning independence and the ability to 'rough it'. She maintains that there is a greater sense of achievement to be had from battling with the elements than winning a computer game[6].

A CHANGE IN TOY CULTURE

Clearly parents are faced with a problem. If their children cannot be allowed to play outside, they need to be kept occupied in the home, and this has led to a considerable change in toy culture. Between 1991 and 1995 there was a 49% increase in the sales of electronic games, and millions of pounds are spent each year on them. Furthermore, nearly half of seven- to ten-year-olds have a television set in their bedrooms (Central Statistical Office).

The change in toy culture is also manifest in a Euromonitor study that highlights a shift away from outdoor communal pursuits to indoor solitary ones. There has been a 12.5% fall in UK sales of equipment such as swings and climbing frames

[6] Dr Elizabeth Newsome 'The Loss of Our Innocence' *The Independent* (15 August 1996)

between 1991 and 1995. Admittedly this was a time of economic recession, but faced with the choice, parents clearly preferred to spend money on toys to occupy their children's minds indoors rather than their whole being outside!

CHANGES IN OUR DEMANDS OF CHILDREN

There is certainly an insidious pressure upon children to grow up, rushing them out of each natural developmental stage into the next. They are presented at an increasingly early age with images of fashion, dining out, needing to look attractive and so on. The former teenage culture has crept lower and lower down the age groups so that now it is to be found in the infant school. This hurry to false maturity is heavily promoted by advertisers who know full well the power of offspring to cajole their parents into spending money. There is no financial gain for the advertisers in children's 'carefree time' spent making mud pies, catching tiddlers or creating home-made camps in trees.

Another very important pressure is placed upon our children in Britain as a result of such an early start in formal education. We are, as far as we can ascertain, the only country in the world where formal education starts at the age of five years. This means that many children are being asked to do things for which they are not yet developmentally ready. A formal start to learning too soon leads to considerable numbers of our children – particularly boys – deciding that education is not for them. Early failure and dissatisfaction is built into the system.

International tables of comparison do not support our practice. Those who enter school at six or seven years, and who have had longer in a nursery setting, actually do better. Furthermore, it is our bottom 40% who present most cause for concern in relation to academic achievement, and it is those children who suffer most from such early demands. National Curriculum testing at six years helps to pile on this pressure.

Finally, a consequence of the recent political desire to provide some form of education for all four-year-olds is that many were absorbed into unsuitable settings. A child who is only just four years is not helped by being placed in an understaffed and overcrowded classroom where individual needs cannot possibly be catered for.

CHANGES IN THE DISTRIBUTION OF INCOME

During the past 20 or so years British society has become increasingly polarised so that the rich became richer and the poor became poorer. Using information from NCH Action for Children and HMSO, Barnardos have calculated that one in four children now live in poverty. While the poor have always been with us, they have never been so exposed to the realities of inequality.

Advertising and the media make children aware of the multiplicity of goods on offer to those who can afford them. It is the job of the advertiser to generate a desire for the material goods he presents. If this desire is frustrated, as in the case of the children of the poor, it will probably lead to a sense of injustice. The 'it's not fair, why can't I have those things?' mentality frequently leads to anti-social attitudes which can, in turn, form the basis for bad behaviour.

2: AN ENABLING ENVIRONMENT

IT IS IMPORTANT TO CONSTRUCT AN ENVIRONMENT that is supportive of children's development as this in itself will avoid many of the frustrations that lead to bad behaviour. Elements of this frustration have been outlined in chapter one, particularly the issue of confinement, and we must compensate as far as we are able by providing a child-centred facility that will enable children's social, emotional, physical and intellectual needs to be met.

We should aim to provide 'can do' situations in 'can do' surroundings. The elements that need to be at the forefront of our planning, therefore, are Time, Space, Resources, People and the Rules that bind them together in harmony.

TIME

If we want to produce children who are capable of exercising such skills as forward planning, implementation (carrying through tasks), concentration and perseverance, it is clearly essential that they must be given blocks of uninterrupted time to pursue their own goals.

It is obvious, however, that no social setting can function without certain time constraints, even if the time constraints are only the beginning and end of each whole session or day. What must be addressed is the question of balance between necessary and unnecessary routines. Unnecessary routines may be in place purely for staff convenience or through force of habit.

Let us assume that uninterrupted blocks of time have been identified. These do have to come to an end. It is essential that endings are prepared for sensitively through staged warnings, for example by announcing three minutes, two minutes, one minute to clearing-up time. Such a warning has the advantage of being objective and begins to provide the children with an understanding of the concept of the passage of time. This will also help them with their personal planning.

SPACE

A child's environment should neither be over- or under-stimulating, and both indoor and outdoor facilities must be considered. A setting which fails to use the outdoors for a considerable part of each day is not meeting all the children's needs nor compensating for the confinement they suffer in other environments.

Features that need to be considered are:

Outside:

- *Safety, cleanliness and security*

- *Physical challenge*

- *Intellectual challenge*

- *Social interaction*

- *Storage*

- *Natural world*

- *Manufactured elements*

- *Opportunities for exploration and discovery*

- *Creative and imaginative outlets*

- *Quiet places for observation and reflection*

- *Variety of levels and surfaces*

- *Pathways*

- *Area markings to facilitate individual and group games*

- *Areas of sun and shade*

- *Gardening, harvesting and habitat*

- *Use of the wider environment including buildings, people, work, transport, parks, gardens and so on.*

Inside:

- *All the features listed above, except for the last four, equally apply to the inside. However, specific consideration should be given to:*

  - *The relationship of one activity to another, for example book corners need to be away from noisy activities*

  - *Sound absorbing materials to promote a quieter working space more conducive to purposeful play*

  - *Display areas, both vertical and horizontal, to exhibit items that will stimulate and satisfy curiosity and encourage contributions from children to promote their self-esteem*

RESOURCES

A 'can do' environment that fosters independence needs resources (that can be used safely) to be readily accessible to the children – children should not need to ask an adult to get equipment for them or to ask permission to use equipment. This means that storage furniture should be labelled commensurate with children's ages and stages. For example, a box of Lego should have a picture of a piece of Lego and the word Lego on the outside for easy recognition.

Resources that are out on display, such as water play equipment, may benefit from a background silhouette for immediate identification and matching.

Many smaller items such as paintbrushes and pencils can be openly displayed in suitable containers for ease of access. Clothing, both personal and communal, should be hung on hooks or pegs at the right level for the children and be labelled.

Giving this freedom of access to the children also involves giving some responsibility for maintaining the resources, both for themselves and others. A simple code of 'Get it, Use it, Return it' promotes personal and social responsibility.

PEOPLE

All the people connected with a setting – employees, visitors and friends – need to be aware of their responsibility as role models. So manners, speech, body language, willingness to help and care and consideration towards others are all important.

Adults are there to:

- *Support children in achieving individual goals*

- *Devise activities to educate them*

- *Maintain the quality and safety of the environment*

- *Establish and maintain a framework for acceptable behaviour*

This leads us on to the question of establishing appropriate and well understood rules that embody personal conduct, care and respect for other people and animals, and responsibility for property and the environment. A more detailed look at rules is provided in chapter 5 on creating and implementing a behaviour policy.

3: AN EXPRESSIVE CURRICULUM

IN RELATION TO CHILDREN'S BEHAVIOUR and their social and emotional development it is vital that the aesthetic, creative and physical sides of their natures are allowed full range and exploration. This will enable children to begin to understand and develop their own self-control and self-awareness, which should in turn lead to happy, balanced young individuals.

What is an expressive curriculum? It is the elements of learning that feed the imagination, wonderment and physical expression of the wide range of human feelings from deepest sorrow to great joy, from the isolation of the individual to the effective group member. How do we provide for the development of these emotions? Let us look at areas within young children's experience.

ART

There are many expressive media that can be used in art, but two of the most common and flexible are painting and modelling.

Painting

The most common form of painting that springs to mind in early years settings uses powder paints and brushes on sugar paper. This form of painting is very valuable – it allows children freedom to portray significant images in colours of their choice. It gives them some control over what they have seen or heard by putting images on paper that determine the size and importance of living beings or inanimate objects in their lives. Children may or may not wish to speak about their paintings. Adults should understand this and be careful not to insist that a child always discusses his work with them. Painting can be explored further if the children are given different kinds of paints, brushes, paper and other materials to paint with and on. The materials can be presented in different ways on different occasions, for example the paper could be flat on the table during one session and clipped on to an easel during another session. By extending the painting materials, adults can introduce more descriptive words. This will extend the children's vocabulary and enable them to express themselves more easily. A wider vocabulary will encourage the children to express themselves in collaborative painting activities, too. Painting can also be ephemeral or more permanent as in finger painting. Here,

children can absorb themselves in pattern and picture making, having complete control over whether they keep their images by printing them off or rubbing them out. This gives children the power to be in control in a very calm situation.

Modelling

There is a variety of media that can be used for modelling, including salt dough, Plasticene®, Playdough, natural materials (sand, earth, wood) and, most importantly, clay. Clay has certain elements that are invaluable in learning to understand change, to be in control of change, and also to understand that materials can be indestructible in one form but fragile in another. Children can also express emotions when working with clay – they can express anger by banging soft clay and enjoy feeling in control when modelling and remodelling objects in clay. By firing clay, children can discover first-hand that the clay has lost its malleable property and that it is now hard and breakable. They learn that the objects they have created in clay now have a permanent shape and have to be treated with care.

Both in painting and modelling, children must learn to care

for the equipment. Then others can use it, share the materials and look after themselves and the environment, keeping as clean as is sensible in the circumstances. Adults must allow children to make a mess and explore fully what they are doing, but equally the responsibility for clearing up the mess must be part of the whole experience.

MUSIC

Music can be exciting, lively, happy, sad, frightening, slow, or fast. There are probably as many words to express music as there are emotions. We do not have to be musicians to experience those feelings. What we must provide for children, though, is a variety of music to reflect different emotions and the opportunity to express themselves through making music or moving in response to it. Here the important element is a wide range both in mood, type and tradition. If we provide children with unlimited background music, they begin not to 'hear' it and fail to respond in any way except by ignoring it. This is not healthy for their emotional or even intellectual development. Music should be chosen wisely and played for a purpose and children helped to discriminate between rhythm, pitch and volume. They should also be encouraged to respond to what they hear, learning to use music as a creative outlet for their own feelings.

Children's response to music can be to join in through song or rhythm, to sit or lie still and listen, to move freely or experience the discipline of a dance pattern. Whatever their response is, while responding to music, children may relax and 'lose themselves' to the music or develop a sense of group identity through dance or song. Such experiences form an essential basis for children's creativity in music-making. For this to develop further a wide variety of both commercial and home-made musical instruments must be available. From simply making sounds to telling stories to their music patterning, children can express their deepest feelings.

PHYSICAL

Expression through physical movement has been touched on in response to music, but it is also important that children have every opportunity to make physical responses to their emotions in our increasingly sedentary lives. Not only do they need to be physical, but they need to learn how to control their responses to anger, pleasure, fear, excitement and so on. To foster this control, there should be provision that is both structured and unstructured. Through dance and drama led by an adult, children can be helped to control their bodies, express moods, work individually or in groups, travel through a storyline to a conclusion or follow their own imaginations, and develop their language. Children also need outside space that is safe but challenging, to let off steam, explore their physical capabilities, learn to mix in small or large groups and share the resources co-operatively. Without this opportunity to be free, we cannot expect children to adjust to the quieter more controlled responses to emotions and turn these into creativity.

NATURAL WORLD

It is important that children can experience and respond to the natural world and see themselves as part of the continuity of life. They need to have living things to take care and responsibility for and to realise that without their attention domestic animals and plants could die. In turn children will come to see how people need to care for themselves and others. Working outside through digging, planting, tending and harvesting food will also teach them patience and a sense of success as a result of their labours. Gradually, they will learn to defer gratification.

ROLE PLAY AND STORIES

Role play usually takes place in some kind of home corner, and is valuable in enabling children to re-create and come to terms with their own home circumstances. The home corner can also be changed into different environments, such as an office, station or hospital, so children can develop their understanding of adult roles and life around them. Using their imagination in these settings, children create relationships and learn to work co-operatively. Role play can also occur outside on a much larger scale, when climbing frames become 'buildings', or bushes become dens. It is vital that adults allow children the space and time to create their own characters in these circumstances but be on hand to help when necessary. This help may be in the form of arbitration, addition or subtraction of materials or extending knowledge and understanding through discussion. Consider the following case study:

CASE STUDY

The following scenario depicts co-operation and negotiating skills as the adult hands over responsibility for conflict resolution to the children, through skillful intervention and discussion.
  Setting: role play
  Dispute: who has the crown
  Actors: two four-year-old girls (Susie and Niru) and one adult

Susie snatches the crown from Niru's head: *'That's mine. I want to be Queen.'* (tears follow).
  Adult *'So you both want to be the queen, but we only have one crown What can we do?'*
  Niru *'But it's mine – I had it first.'*
  Susie *'Yes, but I want one.'*
  Adult (insistently) *'But we only have one crown. We have to do something so you can both enjoy the game.'*
  Niru *'We could make another one with that gold card.'*
  Adult *'What a good idea – I'll help you.'*

Role play often develops naturally into children's own stories, allowing them to verbalise what they have experienced so that they and others can understand the sequence of events. Children need to be exposed to a variety of literature providing the language for them to talk about all kinds of experiences, and understand the pattern of storytelling. The stories must be both imaginative and true-to-life, reflecting all the emotions and social situations that they may meet.

SMALL WORLD PLAY

This is another valuable area that allows children to develop their imagination and act out events with small model versions of real things. Small world play may be a group or solitary activity. It gives children the valuable experience of 'being in charge', playing out emotions, understanding symbolism, developing a story-line and thus verbalising the actions they control.

4: DEVELOPING A SENSE OF RESPONSIBILITY

ACHIEVEMENT ON THE PART OF A CHILD is personally satisfying, but perhaps even more important it earns, or should earn, adult approval and praise. Such acclaim builds a child's self-confidence and self-esteem, and a feeling of emotional well-being, all of which are necessary conditions for happiness and which are highly co-related to positive social attitudes and good behaviour. They produce an 'I can do' mentality that is psychologically healthy and conforms with the innate desire of the young to assume independence and responsibility.

THE NEED FOR PRAISE

The experience of early adult praise and support seems even more important for boys than it is for girls. Boys' egos appear to be more fragile and they are more easily discouraged by initial failure. They will tend to reject those things they are failing at, preferring instead to seek peer acclaim by challenging authority, acting the fool, talking tough or behaving aggressively.

In order to guide children towards success, adults should use their knowledge and expertise to judge the amount of time allowed for free choice within a safe and organised environment. Choice itself demands a measure of responsibility. Those who are always told what to do and are denied the right to decide for themselves are likely to lack initiative, independence and judgement. They can, at worst, become dangerously compliant to authority. Moreover, self-set goals are normally within the capacity of the individual to achieve. When one considers that the environment in which the child operates has itself been controlled by adults (who should have faith in their judgement) then whatever the child chooses ought to be profitable. Children's time should be balanced between being directed and choosing for themselves.

SUPPORTING CHILDREN IN ACHIEVING GOALS

Children should be encouraged to think about what they wish to achieve. More lengthy or complicated activities need planning. Adults should make reference to planning in relation to an organised activity; stating the aim and sequence of events and pointing out materials and equipment that will be used. They should also support individual children by helping them through discussion to think about:

- *What outcome is required?*

- *What materials/equipment are needed?*

- *Where are these to be found?*

- *Where will the activity be carried out?*

- *Is any preparation needed? For example, putting on an apron.*

- *What can/shall they do after the activity?*

- *Should tangible results be displayed, stored or recorded in some way?*

- *Tidying up.*

Such discussions help a child envisage, sequence logically, and consider problems before they happen (and perhaps avoid them). Importantly, they demonstrate adult interest and support. There should be a review at the end of the activity. Discussions like this also do much to develop language that empowers the child to use his intellect rather than resort to an undesirable aggressive response born of frustration when things go wrong.

Children who have learned to behave responsibly will undoubtedly get more out of their education and are likely to enjoy relationships and their work much more than those who have not. The adult responsibility here is very important.

It goes without saying that all acts that reflect a sense of responsibility should be the subject of generous praise.

We can divide the nature of responsibility into four categories:

Responsibility for self

Children need to assume responsibility for themselves as individuals. There are a variety of ways in which this can be done:

● *Personal hygiene – children should wash their hands before meals or cooking activities and after going to the toilet or handling things which could possibly carry bacteria.*

● *Children should be made aware of and increasingly assume responsibility for putting on aprons when engaging in painting, water play or cooking.*

● *They should know the place for personal belongings such as coats and shoe bags and use them properly.*

● *It is important that during parts of the day, children should be free to determine for themselves which activities they undertake and be encouraged to evaluate what they have done.*

● *They should clear up for themselves after activities.*

Responsibility for the environment

It is never too soon to encourage children to take responsibility for aspects of the environment. Here are some things you can talk about and develop with children:

● *Recognising that living things brought into the nursery or nursery garden are entirely dependent on us for their welfare. Children should take part in housing, feeding, watering and the careful handling of animals, as well as cultivating plants.*

● *Giving children opportunities to choose the theme and furnishings in the home corner.*

● *Locating, using and returning items to their correct place.*

● *Helping to prepare for activities by mixing paint or covering tables before craft activities and so on.*

● *Contributing ideas for and helping to mount displays.*

● *Creating and maintaining habitats for animals in the nursery garden.*

● *Encouraging and caring for wild birds.*

● *Using the litter baskets.*

● *Helping to maintain resources in good order.*

Responsibility for others

Let us consider different activities which involve responsibility for others. At this stage in children's development 'others' might include dolls and toys which they imbue with human characteristics. Such activities might include:

● *Caring roles in the home corner – parenting, providing medical treatment, veterinary treatment, looking after visitors.*

● *Comforting other children or toys in an imaginary situation who may be upset or have hurt themselves.*

● *Making items for the pleasure of other people – Mother's/Father's day cards, little gifts for people who have helped them, presents for friends and so on.*

● *Helping people relay verbal or written messages from one part of the nursery to another.*

● *Telephoning (real or imagined) people who may be unwell and asking how they are.*

● *Dictating or 'writing' letters of comfort or pleasure to people.*

● *Dictating or 'writing' thank you letters.*

● *Talking at group time about people who help us.*

● *Discussing characters in stories who have shown kindness to others.*

● *Using 'need narratives' – stories where a need is identified and where children discuss how they can meet that need, for example a teddy bear who has travelled from France and has lost his way. The teddy bear could be very cold, tired and hungry. When the children have suggested how they can help the teddy bear with these needs they can then think of ways he could get home.*

Of course, the successful outcome of 'need-narrative' activities will depend on the skill of the storyteller and her subsequent presentation of need, willingness to consider all the children's suggestions and creation of opportunities for them to actually make things to help the bear.

Shared responsibility
Here it is important that each child plays his part in order to achieve the common goal. We give, as an example, an activity that is likely to take place in all settings – snack time.

What is described is well within children's competence and offers a first-class opportunity for all members of the group to see the importance of their own role for a successful and enjoyable outcome.

PREPARING FOR SNACK TIME

By dividing up snack-time tasks into discrete units, in what can be called 'a system', members of the group assume their essential roles. Each unit can be printed on to a card with an illustration to symbolise it. The cards can be laminated to protect them and placed in a 'preparing for snack time' container. Children can pick out cards from the container in lucky-dip fashion. The units could be as follows:

● *The cloth* – select one from the drawer and lay it on the table. At the end of snack time, brush off any crumbs. If the cloth is clean it can be used again. Fold it up and put it away in the drawer.

● *The table decoration* – you can choose the table decoration. You could have flowers or you could choose a decoration from the drawer and bring it to the table. Clear the decoration away at the end of snack time.

● *The invitations* – take the name cards and invite all the people in your group to come and sit at the table. Put the name cards away at the end of snack time.

● *The drink* – collect the jugs of drink and bring them to the table. Now collect as many cups as you need. Ask everybody what they would like to drink and pour out the drinks they choose. Clear away the cups and jugs at the end of snack time.

● *The snack* – prepare the snack and put it on to plates. Make sure there is a plate for everyone. Hand round the snacks to the group asking people what they would like. Clear away the plates at the end.

Of course, before introducing such a system, the adult will have to talk through what each card is asking the children to do. With daily use it will not be long before the children can 'read' the instructions for themselves.

The advantages of such an organisation are:

- *It involves no favouritism on the part of the adults.*

- *Everybody gets to have a go at everything over time.*

- *The group will appreciate that the pleasurable outcomes of snack time depend on individuals sharing responsibilities.*

- *The activity is part of the 'real world of work' at an appropriate level. Such 'real' experiences are too often denied children nowadays.*

- *If adults involve themselves skilfully in this task then aspects of all areas of your early years guidelines will be covered to some degreee.*

5: CREATING AND IMPLEMENTING A BEHAVIOUR POLICY

To ensure children develop positive behaviour it is essential that the adults they spend time with are good role models – the adults' behaviour needs to be consistently positive and the standards of behaviour they expect from the children should not be impossibly high. By creating and implementing a behaviour policy, adults will be forced to think very carefully about their behaviour and what they expect from the children. This will help adults to create a positive environment that fosters good behaviour.

In this chapter we look at the main elements of a behaviour policy, and provide an example policy to use as a starting point for creating you own policy. It is essential that you create your own policy based on the specific needs of your setting and that you review it regularly.

FEATURES OF A BEHAVIOUR POLICY

Before introducing a behaviour policy, you need to spend time thinking about how it will be interpreted and implemented. A workable behaviour policy should have the following underlying features:

- *It was created by all the adults concerned with the children.*

- *It is realistic in its demands – based on a sound understanding of child development.*

● *It is understood by all concerned – staff, parents, visitors and students.*

● *It is communicated effectively to the children.*

● *It is implemented consistently and fairly.*

● *It affords opportunities for children to exercise some choice within the defined framework.*

● *It is regularly reviewed.*

● *It is capable of recognising that individual children will learn to conform to its expectations at different rates based upon their nature, experience and cultural background.*

UNDERLYING PRINCIPLES

The behaviour policy itself must be explicit and based upon the following rules:

● *Not hurting others.*

● *Not saying unkind things.*

● *Not taking or damaging other people's property.*

● *Not harming any features of the environment, particularly living things.*

● *Not offending others through bad manners.*

A POSITIVE APPROACH

We believe, however, that any behaviour policy is likely to be more effective if it is based upon a positive viewpoint and focuses upon actions and behaviour we wish to instil. Let's turn

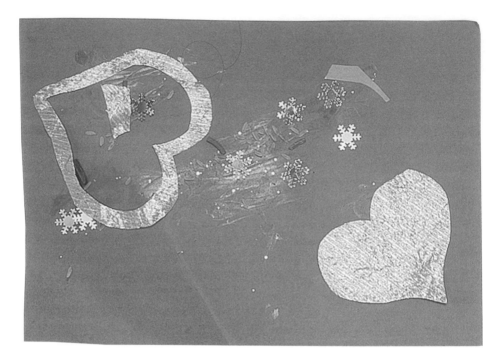

the rules around to read more positively:

- *We always try to be kind to others.*

- *We always try to speak nicely to one another.*

- *We look after our own and other people's things.*

- *We take care of our home/nursery.*

- *We put things back where they belong.*

- *We look after living things.*

These positive statements are few in number and easily understood. Too many rules confuse and often lead to nagging, which is counter-productive.

We must always remember:
When a child transgresses, we condemn the behaviour not the child.

AN EXAMPLE BEHAVIOUR POLICY

The following example policy embraces all the principles professionals need to consider when writing and implementing a behaviour policy. It is essential to remember, however, that every setting will need to form its own policy with its specific needs in mind. It is this process of team discussion that will provide the underlying understanding and sense of ownership. This should lead to consistency in the application of the policy. You could use this example policy as a basis for creating your own. Let's look at underlying principles of the example policy.

Principles of the behaviour policy

- *We recognise the individuality of all our children.*

- *We work in partnership with the children's families.*

- *All adults concerned with the children accept their responsibility for implementing the goals enshrined in the policy.*

- *The policy recognises and will implement the Code of Practice for children with special educational needs when appropriate.*

- *This policy will be regularly reviewed to ensure that any new knowledge will be considered and new circumstances catered for.*

There are four basic principles/rules involved:

- *We look after ourselves (safety and welfare).*

- *We care for others (avoiding actions that might hurt either physically or emotionally).*

- *We all recognise our responsibility in relation to the natural and manufactured world around us.*

- *We respect other people's property and their constructive activities.*

A POSITIVE BEHAVIOUR POLICY

When introducing a behaviour policy, it is vital to ensure that it concentrates on positive behaviour and is not just a list of forbidden activities.

- We do not run indoors.
  We wash our hands before handling food.
  We wash our hands after going to the toilet.
  We clean our teeth after meals.

- We don't hurt other people.
  We don't say and do unkind things.
  We don't throw things (except in ball games).
  We don't push and shove.
  We share things and take turns.

- We look after our animals and plants.
  We put things back when we have finished with them.
  We try not to break things.
  We tidy up after ourselves.

- We do not take things which do not belong to us.
  We do not spoil other people's games.
  We do not spoil other people's things.

It is important to remember that your own actions and behaviour in relation to these principles will communicate their message more strongly than your words. However, it is essential that you explain, comment upon, praise or admonish behaviour when necessary. In this way both your actions and words will be mutually reinforcing and will enable children to begin to internalise a moral code.

Parents must of course be shown this policy and have it explained to them, if necessary. You could also ask parents to sign a contract of agreement stating that they support the behaviour policy in theory and will support it in practice.

6: PARENTS IN PARTNERSHIP

WE CANNOT CONSIDER CHILDREN'S BEHAVIOUR **in isolation – it is inextricably linked to their family circumstances, both influenced by them and influencing them. Indeed, parents and children are just as much the cause of each other's problems as they are of each other's joys.**

PARENTS' NEEDS

Childcare and education professionals are frequently asked for advice and support from parents who, without example from other family members, are often left feeling isolated and confused by the unrelenting demands of their infants. Although some may be 'whizz kids' in information technology or high finance, they can feel at a loss to know what to do with an infant's non-compliance with what they see as quite reasonable requests! Such parents are used to things running smoothly, to being in control of situations and to the kind of predictability which usually goes with efficient organisations.

Other parents find their task daunting for quite different reasons. They may be facing the stresses of financial difficulties, job insecurity or depression. Life for such people is difficult enough without the added burden that parenthood places upon them. There are also some parents who have not had the benefit of good parenting themselves and therefore have little idea of how to interact or play with their children.

TRUST AND UNDERSTANDING

The relationship between professionals and parents needs to be characterised by trust and understanding. It is important for professionals to give any advice and support with extreme sensitivity and to remind themselves that, unlike parents:

● *Professionals have received, or are receiving, training for the work they do.*

● *Professionals work in a child-centred environment with lots of toys, planned activities, materials and equipment that holds special appeal to children.*

● *Professionals have clearly defined hours of work and can go home at the end of the day – unlike parents who have ultimate responsibility for their offspring 24 hours a day, 7 days a week for at least 18 years!*

● *Professionals work in teams and have a lot of colleague support.*

SUPPORTING PARENTS

There are a number of ways in which support can be given to parents without seeming to preach. Success is more likely if professionals generate confidence and encourage parents to trust their own instincts, judgement and common sense. We should help to demystify bringing up children. After all, humanity has come this far reasonably successfully! So, what can professionals do to help those who look to us?

Variety of activities
You can encourage parents to come into your setting to see the kind of things children play and work with – water, cardboard boxes, digging in the earth, rolling out pastry and so on. You can explain how these activities engage children's attention, that they are not expensive to introduce at home and that busy little

people are much less likely to be naughty.

You can show how you are relaxed with the children, how you discuss things with them and offer choice and freedom within a framework of discipline.

Parent groups

You can organise a parents' group which meets regularly and at suitable times. (For those who do not work this will probably be best when their children are actually in the setting, during the day. For working parents evenings may be the best time.)

Parents will find just meeting and talking to other adults in similar circumstances helpful. Whether they choose to focus their discussion on a particular topic or whether discussion naturally ensues around other activities (for example fund raising) should be a matter for the parents. Some parents may welcome professionals joining in the group in an informal manner.

Topic sessions

You can run a session for parents devoted to a topic of their choice relating to children's behaviour. The meeting could include a talk from an invited speaker, with opportunities for questions afterwards. Or parents could ask a panel of experts questions. In either case it is always a good idea if parents write down their questions in advance and hand them in anonymously because:

● *The questions can be shared out and answered by the best person.*

● *Parents will have had time to think of the most pressing question facing them and phrase it in the most appropriate and effective way.*

● *You avoid possible embarrassing silences and situations where parents would like to ask questions but don't dare in case they sound 'silly'.*

You can also set up regular discussion sessions run by the manager and/or staff on a series of common topics that worry parents. These may include:

● *Temper tantrums*

● *Aggression towards siblings*

● *Bedtimes*

● *Jealousy*

● *Confrontations/failure to obey*

● *Meal times/eating*

● *Being rude to other people, perhaps using bad language*

Developing a behaviour policy together

You can work with parents to set up a joint behaviour policy to ensure consistency between all

the significant adults in a
child's life.

You could start the session by showing the group the existing
behaviour policy. The parents should be consulted and asked for
suggestions on reviewing the policy. If you don't have a behviour
policy, use the exmaple policy on page 30 as a starting point.
You should talk about the need for consistency in the adults'
behaviour and how this helps the children's moral development.

Parents will need to understand the underlying principles of a
behaviour policy and the key factors to consider. Make sure they
know and understand the following:

- *Children need praise and feel loved when they receive it.*

- *They do not like criticism, it is isolating and unpleasant.*

- *Over time they learn which actions are praised and which
are criticised.*

You should explain how each child relates to a behaviour
policy and how his understanding develops. Explain that each
child absorbs the information in the policy and translates it into

his own ethical framework. You can often tell when this is beginning to happen by his reactions to the behaviour of friends in a real life situation. In play you may hear his judgements expressed on the 'behaviour' of dolls, toys or even the family pets!

This ethical framework is internalised and becomes an individual's conscience. It is a kind of internal policeman forbidding some actions which are potentially pleasurable and commanding that others be done out of a sense of obligation. Internal policemen are, of course, much more effective in controlling behaviour than other forms of discipline. A well-balanced individual needs a 'policeman' who is neither so strict as to create anxiety nor too permissive! Looking back at the first two statements it must be clear to everybody that it is a lot easier to sort out an ethical framework if all the adults in a child's life praise and criticise the same actions.

Discussing views on behaviour

In addition to or instead of reviewing the behaviour policy, you could hold sessions with parents to discuss general attitudes to discipline. You could introduce the following stereotype views of behaviour as a starting point to talking about good practice.

GENERAL VIEWS ON DISCIPLINE

View A

'Children need a clearly defined framework of what is and what is not acceptable. We need to explain clearly why we ask them to do or not do certain things. We should expect them to conform – in a kindly way of course – and if they transgress then they should be appropriately punished.'

View B

'It's best not to always moan. Children should be allowed to do what they want within reason. If you're too strict and inflexible , you'll end up with timorous little mice with no guts or initiative – you know, the sort of people who follow authority blindly.'

VIEWS ON BEDTIME DISCIPLINE

View A

'Bedtime should be a set routine. It should be at the same time every night, preceded by a bath or wash and teeth cleaning. Then the parents should read the child a story, kiss him goodnight and then lights out. That's the end of the story. Parents need a little bit of time to themselves to relax and do what they want to do.'

View B

'It's just not worth having arguments over such trivial matters as bedtime. Children will want to go to bed when they are tired, then there's no hassle which is bad for both the parents and the child.'

Common sense points to add here:

- Plenty of fresh air and physical exercise are good for children and will make them tired and more likely to sleep!

- Try not to have too many rules. Decide what really matters to you and stick to it.

- Give children some choices within the general rule, for example 'Would you like me to read "The Three Bears" or "Little Red Riding Hood" when you go to bed?'

PERSONAL AND SOCIAL DEVELOPMENT

So far, we have been talking about settings working with their parent body on general issues of children's behaviour. Now we need to look at the way professionals and parents can work together on a more intimate one-to-one basis.

As part of general good practice there should be an easy, informal relationship where either party can raise issues of concern at any time. In addition to this, both parties should be adding their observations to a child's record and this record should include the heading Personal and Social Development. All early years guidelines highlight this most important area of a child's development. We have listed the elements of Personal and Social Development in the English guidelines (Desirable Outcomes for Children's Learning on Entering Compulsory Education 1996 published by SCAA now QCA). The other early years guidelines follow very similar principles. For more information see chapter seven.

Personal and Social Development

- Have confidence and self respect.

- Behave in appropriate ways.

- Be aware of right and wrong.

- Work well in groups and be willing to take turns and share fairly.

- Treat living things, property and their environment with care and concern.

- Have good relationships with and sensitivity to others, including those of different cultures and beliefs.

- Show a range of feelings such as wonder, joy or sorrow.

- Respond to cultural and religious events.

- Concentrate and persevere.

- Take initiative.

- Be able to select an activity or resources.

- Work well independently .

- Have personal independence (for example in dressing, hygiene).

These recorded observations should be the subject of formal discussion and ways ahead sought so that children's development in this area can proceed satisfactorily.

CAUSES FOR CONCERN

In some cases the observations of either or both parties may highlight causes for concern with regard to children's behaviour. Such causes for concern, if they stem from psychological or often more physiologically-based conditions will constitute the first stage of a special educational needs (SEN) procedure and should be entered on your SEN register. Put the emphasis on the concerns that are in the child's interest and add any information parents have that may throw light on a condition, for example general health or traumatic circumstances, which will be helpful in building up a general picture.

You can then work together keeping detailed observations under the following suggested format:

Observation

Name: Date of birth:

Date: Day of week: Time:

Others Present:

Situation:

Observed Behaviour:

It may be that the observations you are both keeping highlight a pattern and even a causal link with bad behaviour. If so, action can be taken to avoid the triggering circumstances. In any case, such observation will form a very useful basis for discussion with any other professionals who may need to become involved in the future.

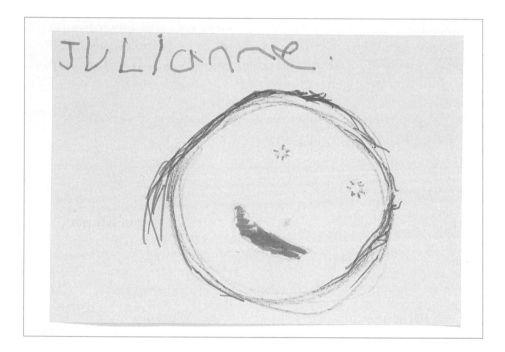

At this stage you will meet regularly to review progress and if, after two such reviews, the child's behaviour has improved you may, with luck, find that the child no longer has a special educational need and that all is now well. However, you should keep the child's name on your register until you are certain that this is the case. If there has been no improvement in the situation, or it has worsened you may feel that you need to move to stage two. You will work closely with parents again and advise them that you intend to draw up an Individual Education Plan for their child to help him. You will also, together, need to gather all the information you can from other agencies – Social Services and/or Health Services may be involved. You will also need to ask parents for any advice that their General Practioner may have to offer. It is possible that Social Services may have concerns about the child's welfare and in very serious cases the child may be on the Child Protection Register. The Local Authority may be responsible for him under the terms of the Children's Act. The setting responsible for the care and education of the child may need additional help through, for example, a pre-school special needs counsellor, an educational psychologist or a health visitor. Aim to hold reviews with the child's parents at least once every 12 weeks. If no progress is being made then the whole procedure goes a stage further to bring in an outside specialist. This is likely to be an educational psychologist, and he or she will make a formal assessment of the child's needs.

At all times, you will be working closely with parents and putting advice received from other specialists into practice. Again, you will be meeting regularly with them to review progress. Good progress may mean that the child can revert to stage two. It is unlikely that pre-school settings will deal with stages four or five. In the case of stage five, a legally binding statement of Special Educational Needs (SEN) is issued and provision to meet these must be made.

Further helpful information on procedures for SEN is available free from the Department for Education and Employment (DfEE). If you telephone 0171 510 0150, the DfEE will send you a book, 'Special Educational Needs Code of Practice'. The circular 'The Education of Children with Educational and Behavioural Difficulties' is also obtainable free from the DfEE.

7: PERSONAL AND SOCIAL DEVELOPMENT

PERSONAL AND SOCIAL DEVELOPMENT is the most important part of a child's development and should therefore have the most emphasis. We have taken the 13 criteria identified in the English guidelines – Desirable Outcomes for Children's Learning on Entering Compulsory Education – published by the School Curriculum and Assessment Authority (SCAA) now the Qualifications and Curriculum Authority (QCA) and shown how you can promote this area of learning. Personal and social development lays the foundations from which all other learning can take place. It is about being able to take advantage of one's education and being a happy and fulfilled person.

This area of learning is very much concerned with good behaviour through promoting children's emotional well-being and ability to enjoy successful social relationships, developing independence and the cultural, spiritual and moral dimensions of their character.

TO HAVE CONFIDENCE AND SELF RESPECT

● Design each child's learning programme so that it embodies challenge yet is achievable.

● Discuss a child's achievements with him directly and in front of his peers and parents when he is present.

● Display work. Where work is not of a permanent nature, as in block constructions for example, photograph the child beside the work and incorporate the photograph into a display.

● Listen attentively to what the child says and make reference to it in later conversations – thus demonstrating real interest.

● Sometimes provide a running commentary on what the child is doing – this shows you're interested and helps with language development.

● Ask the child for his opinion and ideas.

● Ask the child to help you or others.

● Celebrate the children's birthdays.

● Reward children regularly with stickers and symbols to represent good behaviour.

TO BEHAVE IN APPROPRIATE WAYS

● Make sure children know and understand the nursery's code of behaviour (Behaviour Policy).

● Uphold your policy fairly and consistently – have your parents 'on board'.

● Praise good behaviour.

● Be good role models.

● Discuss right and wrong in appropriate contexts as they arise in the nursery.

● Avoid trouble by being well organised – don't let children get bored, plan effectively and get your groupings right.

● Recognise the value of role play in helping children to find their own solutions to problems – only step in if you must.

● Give reasons for your judgments where conflict occurs.

● Where bad behaviour exists explain why it cannot be tolerated – speak quietly, slowly and firmly and insist that the child gives you eye contact.

● Encourage children to understand the consequences of their actions.

TO BE AWARE OF RIGHT AND WRONG

The concept of right and wrong develops slowly throughout childhood. The famous developmental psychologist Jean Piaget conducted an experiment on children's moral understanding. It consisted of telling stories and asking children to say which characters were the naughtiest. The experiment revealed that up to the age of nine or ten years, children tend to see the degree of naughtiness in terms of consequences rather than the intentions of the perpetrator. Thus a child who accidentally broke 15 cups was seen (by a six-year-old) as deserving more severe punishment than another who was engaged in (illicitly) taking jam while his mother was out and breaking one cup in the process.

Our role in helping children understand right and wrong is helped by:

● The wise use of literature, television and so on

● Discussions

● Being very positive when right is done and condemning wrong actions – NOT the children who do them.

TO WORK WELL IN GROUPS AND BE WILLING TO TAKE TURNS AND SHARE FAIRLY

● Have appropriate group size and composition when planning activities. Some children work well together while others don't.

● Play games involving taking turns including boardgames and simple team games with small equipment outside.

● Make sure that 'prestigious' items, such as bicycles and computers are shared fairly. Use name lists to ensure everyone who wants a turn in an activity has one. Timers are useful to ensure fairness.

● At circle time, share out fairly food prepared during cooking activities, snacks and so on. Always make reference to the importance of fairness when cutting fruit or cakes.

● Plan group activities that require the children's co-operation to ensure a successful outcome, such as painting a large model, ring games, and making music.

● Have resources that demand co-operation, for example large wheeled vehicles, group block play and ball games.

● Remember the value of the home corner for introducing situations where co-operation is essential.

TO TREAT LIVING THINGS, PROPERTY AND THEIR ENVIRONMENT WITH CARE AND CONCERN

● Ensure living things are a regular feature in your setting. Animals need not be long-term residents – mini beasts, fish, wild birds in the nursery garden do not need much upkeep.

● Make sure that any animals are kept and housed in a manner that conforms to health and safety requirements.

● Emphasise the responsibility we have for looking after animals and their dependency upon us for their welfare.

● Talk about the need to provide living conditions that match, as closely as possible, the animal's natural environment.

● Provide places where individuals can store their own property.

● Insist on a 'borrow it, use it and return it' policy for reusable items.

● Insist on children using space responsibly for example, preparing tables for painting and tidying up after themselves.

● Take children on walks around the locality and point out evidence of care within it as well as interesting natural phenomena.

- Have nursery collections of suitable materials for recycling.

- Remind children to always throw rubbish away in appropriate places, such as rubbish bins.

- Use designated parts of the nursery garden for cultivation.

TO HAVE GOOD RELATIONSHIPS WITH AND SENSITIVITY TO OTHERS, INCLUDING THOSE OF DIFFERENT CULTURES AND BELIEFS

- Ensure good role modelling by staff caring for children, including the way they interact with children's parents.

- Encourage co-operation through planned activities.

- Make reference to the needs and feelings of others in discussions.

- Praise acts of kindness by children.

- Plan for children's natural nurturing instincts by including caring activities in your role-play programme.

- Encourage children to be sympathetic to those who may have hurt themselves or be upset.

- Introduce problem-solving activities that involve making or doing things that meet other people's needs.

- Invite people from other cultures into the nursery to 'show and tell' about their way of life.

- Create whole or part displays that relate to the lives of people from other cultures.

- Correct any unpleasant remarks made about other people.

- Provide resources, including artefacts, dolls, books, music, dressing-up clothes and pictures from other cultures.

- Celebrate a variety of religious and other festivals.

- Point out features in the neighbourhood related to other

cultures, for example places of worship, restaurants or shops.

● Modify the home corner sometimes so that items within it reflect cultural diversity.

● Prepare dishes from other cultures.

● Ensure that all children have equal access to what the nursery offers. Ensure they share responsibilities as well as rights!

TO SHOW A RANGE OF FEELINGS SUCH AS WONDER, JOY OR SORROW

● Stimulate curiosity with items from the natural and manufactured world, including simple mechanisms.

● Encourage detailed observation of natural phenomena.

● Include plenty of opportunities to celebrate within your programme.

● Present a variety of music to match different moods.

● Plan activities that stimulate all of the senses.

● Take children into the wider world – there is so much to wonder at and enjoy. Make sure experiences are coupled with good quality explanation and discussion.

● Recognise that sad things happen. Let children express their grief – it does not help to deny.

● When very sad events occur, such as death or severe illness, allow for the open expression of individual grief.

● Encourage children to think and talk about the feelings of characters in stories.

● Have books within your collection with which children in difficult situations can identify.

- Provide means of expression through plenty of creative work.

- Encourage children to comfort others through making and doing things, for example making 'get well' cards.

TO RESPOND TO CULTURAL AND RELIGIOUS EVENTS

- Celebrate appropriately – make decorative items, cook and enjoy the food, dress up, carry out appropriate aspects of ritual.

- Have or simulate the necessary artefacts to make all this possible.

- Make sure that you are knowledgeable.

- Present appropriate literature.

- Invite people from different cultures and religions into the nursery to talk to the children about their way of life, customs and beliefs.

TO CONCENTRATE AND PERSEVERE

- Congratulate children on the completion of tasks.

- Site activities appropriately in relation to one another to avoid unnecessary noise and disturbance.

- Make sure you avoid frustration or interruptions to concentration by having sufficient resources for an activity.

- Intervene when frustration threatens.

- Give sufficient time for children to really 'settle down'.

- At the end of a session put incomplete items, such as half built block buildings, to one side so they can be completed later.

- Encourage parents to value their children's work.

- For some children you will need to stage goals within a task to give them a sense of satisfaction along the way.

● Get group size and composition right.

● Where necessary define the territory of an activity by, for example, having a special mat upon which others should not encroach!

● Make sure activities are worthwhile and achievable.

● Build new skills on a foundation of experience.

● Praise and value what has been achieved by displays, for example, or presentations at circle time.

TO TAKE INITIATIVE

● Provide adequate time for children to make their own choices with regard to the activities they wish to pursue.

● Give children opportunities to choose who they work with.

● Don't let adults over-control the nursery programme or be too bound by timetables and routines.

● Within an adult-led activity, respond to individual children's suggestions and ideas.

TO BE ABLE TO SELECT AN ACTIVITY OR RESOURCES

● Within the constraints of health and safety considerations, make resources available for children to choose and select freely.

● Encourage children to plan their own programme for part of the time. It is a good idea to get them to verbalise this plan and follow it up at the end of the session with discussion – 'how did it go?' They may have something to show you.

● Resources should be stored so that they are easily accessible. They should be at the right height and easy to take.

● Make sure it is clear what each storage box contains – labels that are suitable for all stages of development should have a picture and the name of the item or kinds of items in the box.

- Wherever possible use see-through storage.

- Ensure it is made clear where children should return items so that others can then use them – silhouettes of their shape against the wall to indicate where they belong can be useful.

- Aim to have enough resources to satisfy reasonable demand -- keep an eye out for shortages.

- Make sure you have sufficient 'basic provision' to encourage worthwhile choice.

TO WORK WELL INDEPENDENTLY

- Give each child sufficient space to carry out his work. A 'territory marker' in the form of a mat may be useful to enable an individual to pursue some activities.

- Be responsive to children's own plans and ideas – aim to facilitate rather than block.

- Congratulate independent efforts.

TO HAVE PERSONAL INDEPENDENCE

- Have resources that enable children to practice using various fastening systems, such as lacing and buttons.

- Give children plenty of time to dress themselves for outdoor activities, going home and so on – congratulate successes.

- Have routines for hand washing, teeth cleaning and so on, so children come to regard such practices as part of everyday living.

- Have suitable aprons for messy play and so on that are easy to get and put on.

- Provide sufficient suitable storage for clothing, shoes and personal belongings.

8: SOME CULTURAL INFLUENCES

WE HAVE DISCUSSED ELSEWHERE how home, nursery and the relationship between the two are the paramount influences on children's behaviour. In this chapter we shall be looking at other factors that affect children's behaviour and that tend to assume increasing importance as children grow older.

COMMON FACTORS

As in so many spheres of human activity, the hand-wringing, tut-tutting concern of bystanders seldom achieves much and can even be responsible for the very things these bystanders deplore. What we are advocating is that adults play a more active role in controlling certain cultural influences. Their roles will differ in type and intensity according to individual circumstances. We have chosen to focus on those most likely to affect everybody in a care and education environment and over which we can probably exercise a considerable measure of control. They are:

- *Television/video*

- *Literature*

- *Cultural climate (ethos and resources)*

What can we do in relation to the above?

- *Assess the degree of their impact in our own setting.*

● *Control them ourselves and do our best to ensure that others will do the same in order to maximize their positive side.*

● *Be knowledgeable about them. This will probably mean pre-viewing television programmes while video recording them. It will mean running through software programmes before purchasing/using them, pre-reading the literature you intend to present, and being very selective before buying toys, games, equipment and so on.*

TELEVISION AND VIDEO

The great advantage of recording television programmes is that you can then watch them and judge their suitability in terms of their moral messages and quality of language. It also means that you can think about how you will use a programme. You might choose, in front of very small children, to make a comment like, 'Wasn't that kind of so and so to act in that way?' or, 'That's not a very nice thing to do.' With slightly more mature children you might ask them to make judgements for themselves – 'How did the little boy help his Grandma in the story?' or 'How do you think the little girl felt when the birds helped her?' You will also have time to devise valuable follow-up activities that balance the rather passive nature of television watching.

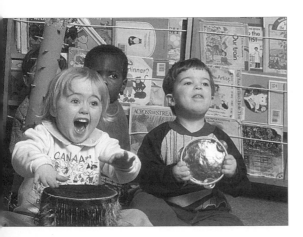

The moving picture holds great fascination for children. It seems to have an almost hypnotic effect on them. Used judiciously, it undoubtedly has great educational value in that it can expose children to environments, cultures, natural phenomena and so on that are normally outside their experience. The sheer range of television coverage has the potential to expand horizons. It may also be useful in increasing children's vocabulary and may expose them to good language modelling. It can explain difficult concepts, often through the use of skillful graphics (this is particularly possible in good computer software). Of course we must not forget the value of television in simply providing enjoyment.

Like so many wonderful things, though, it does have its downside. First, children can become too passive if they watch it a lot. It is one-way communication responsible for all the talking and all the action. Inactivity leaves the abundant energy of young children unspent. This is made worse if the action portrayed causes a flow of unused adrenaline!

A second negative feature of television is its tendency to flit relentlessly from one item to another. A child watching cannot stop it, ask it questions or change in any way what is happening. The rapid transfer from scene to scene – advertisements here, cartoon characters there and documentary material somewhere else – together with the remote control button offering yet more incoherence, is likely to impede children's powers of concentration. Excessive viewing, remote control in hand, often promotes sensation seeking and programmes that do not satisfy this demand may be ignored – encouraging inattentiveness generally. Some professionals in speech therapy and health visiting have noted how the television is never switched off in some homes and blame this among other factors for the increasing numbers of children with speech and language problems.

Dr Sally Ward, an expert in children's speech and language and a respected therapist, has conducted her own research. She has recorded how, whereas over ten years ago the number of children with difficulties was 20%, it is now nearing 40%. Dr Ward's research is pointing the finger at the constant background noise of television. Where this is present adults often do not talk to their children or teach them nursery rhymes and songs. Thus children are not gaining the experience of listening. Without such experience they have difficulty in distinguishing significant foreground noise from unimportant background noise. All this makes the later study of phonics, so important in learning to read, very difficult indeed.

The frequent portrayal of violence or anti-social behaviour is another worrying feature and forms part of an on-going debate about television's role in promoting violence in our society. Research evidence is, at present, rather inconclusive on this issue. However, of the people questioned in a recent *Nursery World* survey on children's behaviour[1], the overwhelming majority (98%) of respondents working in nurseries felt that television characters influenced behaviour. Many television characters behave violently. Interestingly, the research carried out by Lefkowitz et al.[2] found that boys appear to be more influenced by television violence than girls. Whether this is because boys tend to be more aggressive anyway and therefore want to watch such programmes or whether the violent programmes make the boys aggressive is a difficult question to answer.

We believe that violence shown on the screen is much more likely to affect children if it reinforces what they are experiencing already in their life. Moreover, a diet of violence without adult guidance may have the harmful effect of desensitising children so that they are neither shocked by it nor capable of empathising with the victim. Advertisers certainly recognise the power of the medium to persuade the young to purchase their products; if it influences purchasing behaviour, why not other kinds of behaviour?

We have talked about controlling rather than passive acceptance of what's on offer. Aware of the potential positive and negative influences of the medium, we should act upon our knowledge. What can we do? Well, give careful consideration to the following points which should prove useful in putting you in charge:

● *Control the time allowed for watching television, video and so on.*

● *Balance the passivity of television with active, creative and*

[1] R. Andreski, S. Nicholls 'Who's In Control in Your Nursery ?' *Nursery World* (22 August 1996)

[2] Lefkowitz MM et al. 'Growing Up to be Violent' *New York and Oxford Pergamon* (1977)

expressive work. If a programme has stimulated such work then it has been valuable.

- *Exercise your critical judgement about a programme – could its message have been better conveyed in a first-hand mode? For example, why watch bead threading or birds feeding when you can actually thread beads or set up your own bird table? Could you present the message better yourselves?*

- *Allow plenty of time for discussion. Encourage the children to adopt a critical approach to what they are offered. Did they like the programme? Then go into a number of appropriate open-ended questions about it to expand this judgement. Focus particularly on the sayings and doings of the characters in relation to good or bad behaviour. Encourage children to empathise.*

Another very important topic for discussion is whether what is happening is real or fantasy. Small children are often confused over this and muddle the two. Without the guidance of a loving adult to help them sort it out, much fantasy (and often violent) material may be considered 'real' and therefore present the world as a much more violent place than it really is. A child may come to believe that violence and aggression are behaviour one should adopt in order to 'fit in'.

THE IMPORTANCE OF THE LANGUAGE MODEL

Mastery of language increases a child's capacity to think about his actions and their consequences. It therefore aids self-control and encourages communication by words rather than (often violent) actions. Understanding and using language effectively is essential for educational success and so, indirectly, it is tied up with self-esteem. Moreover, behaviour management is helped if we can encourage children to think (for which they usually need language) about their actions and the possible consequences of them. Impulsiveness is a characteristic of the very young so, in effect, we are seeking ways of helping children put language between an initial impulse and the action that follows. But how can we set about doing this?

- *By presenting good language modelling ourselves, speaking clearly and grammatically correctly. When introducing new words we recognise that context will help children to understand their meaning, but we cannot be sure of this. It is therefore important to check for understanding and explain if necessary.*

- *By offering a rich diet of literature.*

- *By encouraging discussion which will involve children in all the main uses of language – making statements, asking questions and issuing commands. They should talk about past and present events and predict happenings in the future.*

● *By inviting people into our setting to talk to children about any number of things from commentaries on the kittens they have brought in to their collection of shells to their hobby of playing the flute.*

● *By affording plenty of time for purposeful play. This in itself generates some of the most valuable opportunities for using language. It is one of the main justifications for play featuring so prominently in early years education.*

The importance of listening

Mention must be made to the importance of listening in all this. Many professionals complain that children find it increasingly difficult to listen these days. One reason for this is undoubtedly the cacophony of noise that fills their environment. However, if they cannot and do not listen, children are excluded from receiving information presented to them through the aural sense. They miss out on vital language modelling and we cannot be sure that they have understood our explanations and injunctions in relation to the behaviour we require. So, as well as doing all of the above to develop language we also need to consider the environment in which language is taking place. Noisy and quiet activities should be separated because discussions and story sessions need to take place in tranquil surroundings.

THE CULTURAL CLIMATE AND ITS INFLUENCE ON CHILDREN'S BEHAVIOUR

We must all be aware of just how important the early years are when shaping children's attitudes. For this reason great emphasis is placed by the regulatory authorities, backed up by legislation, on offering a programme of learning which includes other people's cultures and beliefs. If this did not occur then ensuing ignorance and prejudice can all too early lead to unacceptable behaviour by both groups and individuals.

Tolerance

There are three main reasons why practitioners must get the cultural climate right – to promote tolerance, harmony and inclusion. Through helping children acquire knowledge and understanding about other people, and their culture and religion, and showing that diversity can be both interesting and enriching, we promote tolerance. Tolerance is far more likely to lead to decent behaviour than narrow-minded views which often condemn others.

Harmony

The correct cultural climate helps counteract the tendency all groups have to believe that they and their way of life is superior – and by implication that others are inferior. It helps children to feel in harmony with society. They belong because they see their group and its culture represented and celebrated.

Inclusion

If we turn the situation round and look at the likely consequences of not getting the cultural climate right, we must be struck by the serious nature of the responsibility placed upon us. Intolerance and prejudice so easily leads to ugly bullying behaviour including name calling and physical abuse. Victims feel a smouldering sense of injustice which translates into either withdrawal or combative behaviour.

Feelings of exclusion, as well as damaging an individual's self-image, may also lead to anti-social behaviour. Imagine wanting to paint a picture of your mother and there being no colour or possibility of mixing one that matches her skin tone. Imagine if, among all the images and artefacts around, you could not see anything that relates to the way you look or the things you do. Wouldn't you feel alienated? Indeed, you might even reject such an unpleasant society together with the education it is trying to impart. Is your establishment confident about the measures it employs to promote good behaviour and social harmony among different ethnic groups and a sense of well-being among individuals?

Do you, for example:

- *Celebrate diversity with tastings and feastings of other cultures' food?*

- *Go through your books, artefacts, pictures and so on to make sure that they portray and represent varied cultures and beliefs?*

- *Enable children to try on other people's style of dress, play with their kinds of cookery utensils and put their kinds of dolls to be in the home corner?*

- *Tell stories from varied cultures?*

- *Encourage empathy through discussing issues such as belonging and exclusion?*

- *Play music from a variety of cultures?*

- *Encourage children from different cultural backgrounds to co-operate in pairs and small groups?*

- *Invite representative adults to visit your setting and tell children about the way they do things?*

THE IMPORTANT INFLUENCE OF TRADITIONAL LITERATURE

Modern literature has much to offer in terms of freshness and immediate relevance to children's lives. However, it is imperative that children are exposed to the wealth of traditional literature in the form of fables, folk and fairy tales because:

- *These provide a common cultural heritage which contributes to social cohesion.*

- *They include characters which clearly embody either good or evil – small children cannot cope with shades of grey in this regard.*

- *They present situations where good triumphs over evil.*

- *They do not present an immediate solution to the challenge. In identifying with the characters, children are led to understand that perseverance in the face of dangers and difficulties ultimately succeeds.*

- *The modern tendency of protecting children from the unpleasant and frightening can be counter-productive. By meeting such dangers through literature children will acquire strategies to recognise and cope with them as and when they occur in real life.*

- *Children will learn that time must often elapse before goals can be reached.*

- *Actions, guided by the moral tenet of good winning over evil, will determine 'happy endings'. These in turn present the future in a positive light.*

- *Exposure to such stories helps to build an individual's moral code in preparation for adulthood.*

- *Regular exposure to such stories should help provide children with the emotional security to cope with their own fears.*

9: UNDERLYING CAUSES OF ABNORMAL BEHAVIOUR

IT IS IMPORTANT TO DISTINGUISH between mildly troublesome behaviour, which all children display from time to time, to its more extreme and persistent form. The former may have a variety of causes ranging from tiredness and hunger to the child simply being off colour.

In this chapter we shall explore some of the underlying causes of behaviour that disturbs the harmonious workings of the nursery or the home. One must recognise that many of the causes of difficult behaviour lie outside the nursery, having their origins in the child's family circumstances. Indeed sometimes staff in a nursery may find themselves involved in these circumstances, perhaps being asked for help or advice by the child's parents. In more extreme circumstances, they may be asked to provide evidence before a court if child abuse is suspected.

EXPECTATIONS

Children may behave badly in response to unrealistic expectations on the part of those who care for them. Such expectations may take one of two forms. The first reflects a lack of understanding on the part of an adult about children's normal development. The adults do not appreciate that all small children are essentially egocentric and that they cannot, at this stage, be rightfully accused of being spoilt, selfish, bad mannered and so on. Such an adult may expect a child to be good and able to control his emotions, and when such expectations are not met the adult may resort to harsh verbal or even physical punishments. Consider the following opinion:

> ❛ *James is over two years old now. Whenever I take him to the shops he shows me up. When I'm standing talking to my friends he keeps interrupting and pulling my arm for me to get him an ice cream or whatever. If I ask him to wait a minute he only shouts and has a temper tantrum. I often end up smacking his legs. He should be able to do as he's told by now.'*
> Frustrated mother

Another form of unrealistic expectation relates to intellectual achievement. Over-ambitious parents may want to use their children to reflect glory upon themselves – to be a form of status symbol. Sometimes this can become a group phenomenon where different sets of parents vie with each other to see whose child is making the greatest progress in for example literacy or mathematics. Such expectations are harmful for all children, but most of all for those who don't 'shape up' and therefore become aware that they disappoint. Children begin to feel that love is dependent not upon who they are but upon what they can do, often with serious repercussions for their emotional well-being. Consider the following comments:

> ❛ *It's a tough world out there and only the fittest will surive. Jonathan is a bright boy and I want him to be top of the class. He should be reading better than he is now or he'll be left behind.'*
> Ambitious father – MD of a local company

Sometimes expectations are wrong for the opposite reason but with equally serious consequences. A very able or gifted child can become frustrated and badly behaved because not enough is demanded of him. The educational programme may be insufficiently challenging and adult responses to the vast number of questions posed inadequate or non existent. Peers often find such children odd and exclude them socially. This only helps to exacerbate the child's problem. Help in identifying and catering for the special needs of such children can be obtained from The National Association for Gifted Children (see Useful Organisations).

INCONSISTENCY

Inconsistency may occur when two parents have different approaches to discipline as in the comments presented here:

'*Michael is very disruptive in the nursery. Other children do not want to play with him. When he approaches individuals or small groups he wrecks whatever they are doing. When they complain he usually responds by spitting, biting or hair pulling. We have to assign a member of staff to be near him all the time. We are trying to work with his parents but this is not easy. Mum agrees that Michael can be difficult. He takes very little notice of her and she nags him in a quiet voice that rarely alters what he is doing. Then she gives up. Dad, on the other hand, is quite a different kettle of fish. Michael is afraid of him and does his bidding. Dad believes in strict discipline for boys, who he feels need a good hiding from time to time. He proudly boasts, "a good hiding never hurt me". Perhaps it is because he is so authoritarian that Mum gives in to Michael. She says he's too young (at four years) to be expected to do as he's told all the time.*'
Nursery nurse

Another feature of poor parenting is inconsistency in responses towards children's behaviour. If action A elicits a good telling off one day, but is ignored the next, or if action B is praised on one occasion, but receives no attention on another, a child could be forgiven for his confusion and might legitimately ask, 'so what is right and what is wrong?' It might even lead a child to consciously or otherwise check again – perhaps by repeating bad behaviour just to find out! If bad actions are condemned consistently and good ones praised consistently it soon becomes clear to a child how he can gain the praise he so dearly needs to build self-esteem. He will also learn how to avoid criticism, which is often a rather painful experience. In this way behaviour is moulded into an acceptable form.

Parental inconsistency can take another form which is equally confusing to a child, namely, when they say one thing while doing another. They may admonish a child for losing his temper while frequently doing so themselves, in which case it is not surprising if the child becomes rebellious. We have to remember that actions often speak louder than words!

CASE STUDY FOR INCONSISTENCY

Mr and Mrs Jarvison sat down together and decided what their daughter Annabelle should be expected to do in terms of behaviour.

She must always tell the truth
yet:
They told the Headteacher fibs when they said that they kept Annabelle away from school because she had a cold. They really went away for a long weekend.

She must not hurt other people
yet:
They sometimes slap their elder son when he is naughty.

She must share things with others
yet:
They tell the children to go to bed after a very plain tea – the children have seen the strawberries that their parents will eat as a dessert at the evening meal.

Persistent and petty nagging is also harmful, as it builds up a kind of immunity to what is requested by adults. Even worse is harsh discipline, affording little opportunity for the child to make free choices within a reasonable framework of rules, the reasons for which are carefully explained. A small child may respond to such a regime by becoming withdrawn. Conversely he may become rebellious and immune to successive stages in punishment. Shouting progresses to slapping, slapping becomes more severe until ultimately there is nowhere else to go and the child becomes immune to virtually anything the parent says or does.

ROLE MODELS

Children pick up their codes of behaviour and moral values from those around them. If their parents or others close to them are aggressive, abusive, anti-authority, careless about their environment, or cruel in their dealings with other people, then it should not surprise us if their children follow suit. Such children have poor role models because of the example their parents set.

Sometimes parents opt out of role modelling by default. This may be because they are either overworked and have no time or because they are depressed and unable to assume their role properly. Consider the following comments:

Rose is aged two years. The childminder brings her to nursery every day. Rose's parents both work in London and are professional high fliers. Rose seems withdrawn and unhappy. She clings to nursery staff at the end of the day and

clearly does not want to leave. Father is often abroad and mother has left a note on the child's file that she can only be disturbed in the most extreme emergencies as the meetings she leads are vital to the success of the company. She has left the childminder 'in charge' and she is the one who should be contacted.'
Nursery manager

The trouble is, the vacuum created by the absence of their influence has to be filled somehow, in the above case by the childminder. But too often it is filled by the vicarious influences of television or video. Not only are such influences often highly unsuitable, they do, in themselves, need careful discussion and explanation. Without an adult standing by, a young child finds it impossible to sort out fact from fantasy and may be frightened or disturbed by what he sees. The frequent violence portrayed by television characters, even in children's programmes, is often acted out in the nursery or school playground as any childcare professional will testify.

In some cases it may be the insecurity of the parent that leads to the child's problem. The parent may wish to maintain the latter's state of dependency, inhibiting the child's development into a separate human being. In such cases the parent may try to hang on to them as long as possible, exaggerating any minor ailments as a justification for keeping the child at home. All this makes it very difficult for the child to make or keep friends, face up to life's challenges or take the necessary steps to independence. Such children may be the subject of teasing by others for being a 'baby' and may even be bullied. Conisder the following comments:

Mrs P adores Charlie, as she calls him. She has been with him 24 hours a day for the last four years and found it difficult to bring him to nursery and then leave him with us. The health visitor has strongly advised her of the importance of giving Charlie more independence so he can get ready for school. He has very little experience of socialising and finds separation a painful experience. He cries hysterically when his

mum goes and she is obviously very pained by the separation herself. She'll use any excuse to keep him away from nursery.'
Head of nursery

PHYSIOLOGICAL CAUSES

Some causes of worrying behaviour stem from a physiological rather than an emotional cause. Where this is the case, the child will obviously have special needs and require help and support from outside agencies. The nursery staff will have to work closely with parents and such agencies and agree a special programme of education for that particular child.

Although fairly rare, one of these conditions is hyperactivity. A truly hyperactive child is not to be confused with very lively children found at the end of the normal continuum. True hyperactivity is very difficult to deal with.

It is characterised by excessive physical and mental activity. Such children lack concentration, have short attention spans and are always 'on the go'. They often operate on a short fuse and are prone to frequent temper tantrums. To make matters worse for their parents and carers, they do not require much sleep and so are both trying and tiring to look after.

Genuinely hyperactive children require medical treatment. In some cases, most frequently in the United States and Australia, they are treated with drugs to calm them down.

Another disorder that nurseries may encounter is autism or its milder form, Aspergers syndrome. Here again, such children need specialist support. They do not form normal emotional attachments, have severe communication difficulties and normal speech development is impaired. Typically they manifest obsessive behaviour and repeat actions or insist on holding certain objects and carrying them around at all times. Hand flapping is another typical sign of autism.

Another disorder now identified is Attention Deficit Disorder (ADD). ADD is defined by Dr Green of the Royal Alexandra Hospital for Children in Sydney, Australia, as a cluster of different kinds of behaviour such as inattention, poor impulse control, restlessness, disorganisation, poor self-motivation and inappropriate social skills.

The continuing identification of a variety of behavioural disorders underlines that nursery professionals need to keep their knowledge up-to-date through in-service training and professional publications.

DEATH AND SEPARATION

The death of a parent, grandparent, sibling or a family pet is a devastating event in the life of any child and will have inevitable consequences for his or her emotional well-being. Children react to such an event in different ways. They should, however, be allowed to express their grief through whatever means they choose. This may be through quietness, tears, or wishing to talk about it. Others may wish to paint pictures, act out the situation in role play or seek to identify characters in the same situation through stories and books. Consider the following comments:

Melissa's grandmother recently died of cancer. For some time prior to this sad death Melissa had been unhappy – her grandma spent the last three weeks of her life in a Macmillan Hospice. A great air of sadness hangs over Melissa's family. She spends much of her time in nursery quietly playing with the dolls in the home corner or sitting on the settee in the book area. She has ceased to interact with the other children (before this situation arose Melissa was extremely outgoing). We give her as much one to one time as we can and listen sympathetically while she talks about her Grandma. We are always very sensitive when she paints pictures of her and then puts lots of black or dark brown colour in the background. The feeling of loss experienced by Melissa is no doubt made

worse by the fact that Grandma was a very loving primary carer who lived in the family home while Mum worked.'
Nursery key worker

Sometimes children may want to bring in a photograph of the deceased person, pet or something that had belonged to them. Nursery staff should respect such wishes, show an interest in them and talk things over with the child. They should at all costs resist the temptation to try to cheer up the child by saying such things as 'don't cry', 'dry those tears', 'cheer up' or seek to change the subject before the child is ready.

The separation and/or divorce of a child's parents inevitably seriously affects their emotional security. The close bond they have experienced with one parent is shattered and reactions to this vary again. Children may be withdrawn and find it difficult to concentrate or they may behave aggressively and destructively. Support should be provided not only to the child but also to the parent left with prime responsibility for care.

The situation is most damaging where the child is used as a pawn in bitter wranglings. Least harm will be done where both parents seek to reassure him of their love and try, at least in front of him, to co-operate over access. It is so much better if, for example, the parent with responsibility for care and maintenance allows the other to step over the threshold and perhaps have a cup of tea or coffee before taking the child out. The important influence of what the child experiences in relation to what is being said and what is being done is so obvious in the case of his parents. How can he be expected to imbibe into his moral framework the notion of care and kindness for others if he hears it said but experiences quite another reality. Consider the following comments.

We're going to move and my Daddy isn't coming with us. What will my Daddy do on his own? My Mummy says she never wants to see him again 'cause he's a horrible man." Giles (aged almost five years). This devastating news was announced by Giles whose behaviour changed markedly from a sociable,

hardworking little boy to one who is constantly seeking attention and unable to concentrate.'
Nursery nurse

There are other situations where separation from a parent may occur on a temporary basis, but still affect the child's ability to function effectively while he comes to terms with the changes. There may be times when a parent works abroad for a period, for example in the forces or for a multinational company, or where the parent works away during the week returning only at the weekends. The child might live with another parent/stepfamily at the weekend, returning to his 'base' family during the week. A parent, grandparent or sibling might enter hospital or be seriously ill at home, changing the family dynamics during the illness. All these life changes will inevitably affect children's behaviour in some way, and reassurance and empathy are the key elements to maintain – keeping the known environment as safe and as familiar as possible.

In all cases of abnormal behaviour, parents and carers must also examine their own behaviour and ensure they are not affecting negatively the child's reaction to life. Children must also be helped to develop the language to enable them to express their feelings. This will be through role play, story, conversation, explanation, and creative outlets such as music, drama and art.

JEALOUSY

Here, we are talking about an emotional response to another person's perceived favoured position in family relationships. We are all very likely to have had feelings of jealousy at some time in our lives. It is a natural reaction to some changes in relationships, most notably for children with the arrival of a new sibling. It may also exist if parents do not succeed in treating both or all of their children fairly throughout their childhood. Consider the following comments:

 We first noticed something wrong when Lisa began to hit the dolls in the home corner and squeeze their arms ferociously

– at the same time grimacing in such a way as to suggest the considerable force she was exerting. She also tore some of their clothes. We talked to her mother about this and together we came to the conclusion that feelings of jealousy were at the bottom of this behaviour. Mum confesses that she has been "very taken up with the new baby" and the situation has been made worse by the fact that the new baby was premature and therefore needed even more attention than most newborns.'
Nursery key worker

Jealousy is a manifestation of insecurity and unhappiness. To avoid its persistent negative effects adults need to recognise how children may be feeling. They should give them the attention they deserve and reassurance. In the case of a new arrival this is best done by careful preparation before a sibling's birth – including them in sharing information, decisions, practical preparations and so on.

After the birth, the older child should be included, wherever possible, in actual care, or parallel care with dolls. In addition 'special time' should be devoted exclusively to the older child.

CHILD ABUSE

Children may be abused in several ways – emotionally, sexually, physically or through neglect. Sufferers will have varying ways of indicating their unhappiness. They are often anxious and may express this anxiety through aggression, being withdrawn, being tired, or projecting the experience suffered on to dolls, toys, pets or even other children.

In the case of physical abuse there may be signs such as bruising. Nurseries should discreetly seek an explanation from parents about such signs. If staff are not satisfied with the explanation, they must put their child protection procedures into action. Staff will need to sensitively tell the parent(s) that they intend to inform the local social services.

10: TYPES OF BAD BEHAVIOUR

IT IS ESSENTIAL WHEN ADDRESSING the wide spectrum of possible kinds of negative behaviour in children that professionals are aware and communicate to parents that certain kinds of behaviour at certain ages are acceptable, as part of the children's natural development. Other kinds of behaviour are out of the norm and make life difficult for the adults, but first and foremost for the children themselves. It is these kinds of behaviour that are labelled 'bad' or 'unacceptable' and need to be corrected to enable children to develop socially and enjoy life.

MAIN CONCERNS

The readers of *Nursery World* who responded to the survey 'Who's in control?' (22 August 1996) believe that children's behaviour has worsened over the past 10 years. The article 'A turn for the worse' in *Nursery World* (17 October 1996), based on nursery staff responses, listed the kinds of behaviour causing parents most concern, such as temper tantrums. The nursery staff found the most common difficulty they encountered was aggression, or more specifically, biting, disruption of activities, being destructive and then temper tantrums. The survey highlights a number of kinds of behaviour that exist and are unacceptable to our society.

Most common types of bad behaviour
In this chapter we discuss the most common types of bad behaviour and consider how to deal effectively with each one. They are:

- *Temper tantrums.*

- *Aggression – including fighting, biting, spitting, hitting and hair pulling.*

- *Bullying, both physical and verbal.*

- *Destructive behaviour – stopping others' creativity, breaking, throwing, demolishing.*

- *Challenging authority – parents, staff, other adults, older children.*

- *Anti social – unacceptable behaviour in terms of manners, swearing and so on.*

- *Withdrawn – unable to socialise.*

- *Sexually unnatural behaviour.*

- *Mealtime disputes, picky eating.*

- *The child with special educational needs.*

Ground rules

Before we address each type of behaviour there are a number of ground rules that are applicable to every kind of bad behaviour and the way it is managed.

- *Every establishment needs to discuss and agree an effective behaviour policy (see Chapter 5).*

- *The Behaviour Policy must be explained to the parents so that they can reinforce it at home, to avoid children playing*

one group of adults off against another and providing children with consistency.

- *It is the behaviour that must be labelled not the child.*

- *Children must feel valued as individuals.*

- *The emphasis should be on praising good behaviour and ignoring bad behaviour as far as possible.*

- *Always aim to use diversion away from bad behaviour towards something different and positive.*

- *Avoid shouting whenever possible.*

TEMPER TANTRUMS

Temper tantrums are seen as part of growing up and of children establishing their place in the pecking order when they are about two years old. Temper tantrums become unacceptable when they continue to occur in three-, four- and five-year-olds. However, whenever they occur they must be managed and the child helped to come to terms with the situation that sparked off the tantrum. Use the following action plan to help you cope with temper tantrums.

ACTION PLAN FOR DEALING WITH TEMPER TANTRUMS

- The adult must take control and stay calm – adding to the noise and discomfort of the situation by shouting yourself will not help.
- The child must be told calmly and clearly to stop shouting/kicking/crying so that the problem can be resolved.
- Do not at this stage be tempted to bribe the child into quietness by a sweet/treat and so on.
- Tell the child, ' When you are quiet we can talk/cuddle'. It is

important to remember here that temper tantrums occur because the child feels out of control, possibly frightened and may be very tired. In the end the child needs to recognise your love for him and your calm control.

● It may be necessary to walk away from the child having his tantrum but keep him in your sight saying, 'When you have calmed down, I'll come back and we can talk/cuddle'.

● As the child calms down – and the child will eventually – make sure you then give him time to talk/cuddle; ask what the tantrum was about; explain the noise caused by the tantrum upset you, and possibly others, and ask the child to try not to do it again.

● Leave him in no doubt that his behaviour is not acceptable but he is still loved.

● You may find he now needs a rest or to play with something quietly. Temper tantrums often leave children physically exhausted. While the child is recovering you will also need to recover – what about a quiet cup of tea or a few deep breaths!

AGGRESSION

When one child attacks another through fighting, biting, spitting, hitting, hair pulling and so on, he must be left in no doubt that his behaviour is not acceptable. A quick reaction to stop the behaviour by holding the perpetrator's hand and saying 'No, we don't do that here' makes it very clear that the behaviour is disapproved of. What happens next very much depends upon the age of the child and the extent and frequency of the aggression.

Young children under two years need the above step taken and the victim needs to be reassured and checked that he is not hurt. Indeed by giving attention to the victim rather than the perpetrator, we show that aggression does not gain our attention. When the child is over two years old, you need to react to the aggression by encouraging the aggressor to think about how the victim feels. Say 'You would not like it if I did that to you'.

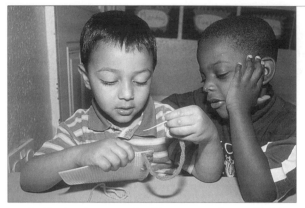

If a child above the age of three years is aggressive towards another it may be necessary to follow up the initial reaction with a 'time out' period, telling him to sit on a chair for a few minutes (in your full view) to underline your deep dislike of the behaviour and then talk to him about how such behaviour hurts.

There is a debate about whether the perpetrator should be made to say 'sorry'. If you do take this line remember it must come from the child's understanding that what he has done is wrong, not just from your insistence that he parrots the words. You can put it another way by suggesting he makes his victim feel better by giving him a hug.

BULLYING

Much has been written on the subject of bullying, particularly in reference to older children, but it is vital to recognise that both verbal and physical bullying is often a learned behaviour. It is important that the environment in which a child finds himself does not present bullying, in any form, as acceptable. This means that all adults must look at their own physical and verbal behaviour towards each other. They should be presenting a caring, supportive environment in which positive relationships are emphasised.

To counteract bullying, bullies and potential bullies must realise that their behaviour will be met with punishment. Underlying causes of bullying should of course, be investigated and dealt with. Victims and potential victims must realise that the adults will take them and their feelings seriously. If you do get a reported incident of bullying it is vital that you act quickly.

Gather as much information as you can about the reported incident, decide whether bullying actually did occur and then speak to the accused child (you may have observed the incident yourself). Do this in a calm but firm manner, taking the child aside, and in turn listen to his explanation. Then explain to the bully why the actions are not acceptable and ask how he would feel if it had happened to him. End the conversation by giving the bully a clear positive message that you still like him, but explain what the penalty would be if it happens again. You must make sure that any penalty is carried out. Idle threats will undermine your behaviour management system.

Efforts must be made to give the victim strategies to tackle the problems themselves by being more assertive.

It is useful to use situations such as role play and story time to emphasise co-operation and play down actions such as bullying.

DESTRUCTIVE BEHAVIOUR

Children who engage in this type of behaviour are usually angry about something – either at themselves, something in their lives or at another person, so they damage items often without thinking why or about the results of their actions. It is important that the adults again intervene both physically and verbally in a calm manner to show the action and its consequences are not acceptable. Also, as in dealing with bullying, adults must explain to the child that he would not like it if it happened to him. Then if it is appropriate, ask the perpetrator to help the other child/ren to put things back where they were or make other appropriate reparation. A moment of 'time out' may also be useful here.

CHALLENGING AUTHORITY

In these situations it is necessary to ask yourself if the authority you're upholding is realistic and practical, otherwise you will only get into a 'no win' situation. The authority you hold comes from sensible rules to ensure safety of the environment and from the respect you command from the children and other adults through your general demeanour and track record of how and why you implement the rules.

Although nursery-age children do not fully understand rules, you can help them to acquire an appreciation of their purpose by, for example, asking them what would happen under the following circumstances (and during the course of actual activities):

• *If when playing a board game one person moved the counter more than the dice indicated that they should.*

• *If at snack time the first person took all the biscuits or fruit for himself.*

• *If in a game of 'Guess which instrument is playing' the blindfolded person peeped.*

When children challenge authority it is necessary to say clearly and calmly:

'No, that is not possible because ...'

'No, you know we don't do that because ...'

'I am asking you to do this because ...'

You will see from these statements it is necessary to take control but explain why you have made the decision. You must then ensure that your request is carried out. If the child fails to comply, you may need to add a threat such as taking away a favourite activity, but ensure that any threat is carried through.

ANTI-SOCIAL BEHAVIOUR

This type of behaviour can only be prevented in an atmosphere where all adults concerned are clear about what is acceptable and what is expected in terms of social manners/behaviour so that the children can be presented with the correct model at all times. Within this atmosphere, they can be told quietly, 'We don't do that or say that here'. It is important for staff to decide which social mores will be encouraged. It is essential that staff remember it is their responsibility to play their part in bringing up children who will find it easy to fit into society as a whole. Failure to do this impedes children's adjustment to life outside the nursery.

WITHDRAWAL

What should staff be doing to help the child who is withdrawn? This kind of behaviour is perhaps even more serious than the overt unacceptable behaviour discussed above. It may be less annoying or less inconveniencing to staff, but a child displaying symptoms of withdrawal could well have deep-seated emotional problems. Any such problems need to be discovered and solutions sought.

A withdrawn child needs his confidence built up by sympathetic staff who encourage him to enter into a variety of social gatherings. This could be by taking the child's hand and working alongside him so he has support and sees how it is possible to engage in activities. Gradually the physical adult support can be withdrawn while verbal support and acclaim is continued until it becomes less necessary. The withdrawn child could be given time to act out possible fears in role play.

SEXUALLY UNNATURAL BEHAVIOUR

Children have to explore the roles of male and female in a variety of play situations. It is here that staff will sometimes see very explicit and perhaps uncomfortable (for them) play evolve.

It should be remembered, however, that strong biologically determined drives often prompt children to explore their own and each others' bodies. Such behaviour is natural and part of growing up. If the behaviour includes practices that children would not know about unless:

- *They had seen them on television or video.*

- *They had seen adults in action.*

- *Adults have involved them in an abusing situation.*

It will be necessary to take prompt action by talking to parents and, if necessary, social services.

In whatever way you need to intervene in such play, it must be done sensitively – have due regard for children's feelings at the time. It could also be harmful for their future psychological well-being in relation to sexual matters if undue attention is drawn to them, with possible resultant feelings of guilt.

MEALTIME DISPUTES, PICKY EATING

This is an area that often concerns parents and by the time they speak to staff at a nursery, mealtimes may have become a battle of wills. In the nursery, staff have a much easier job, as any difficulties with food are not so personalised and the presence of other children who enjoy mealtimes and a variety of food is a great incentive to picky eaters. It is important that mealtimes are presented as a relaxed, enjoyable part of the day where the emphasis is not on the food so much as the social meeting and sharing of the meal. Children should be given some choice as to what is put on their plate and only small portions given at any one time. As the food is eaten, gentle congratulations for clearing his plate or comments such as, 'That was nice, wasn't it?', should follow and then the child should be asked if he wants any more. His favourite food can always be held as a reward for eating something he is not used to. If a child has asked for a certain food he should be encouraged to finish it. Stopping children picking between meals will also help them as they will be more ready to eat at the required time. Do not force a child to eat what he really does not like – we all have our preferences and some foods do honestly make us feel sick!

SPECIAL EDUCATIONAL NEEDS

A child with special educational needs should not be seen as one who automatically presents bad behaviour. But his condition may mean his behaviour is not as acceptable as that of the majority of children and so careful consideration of how these children are supported must be part of their programme.

To achieve a stepped programme of support as presented in the five stages of the Code of Practice (DfEE 1994) observation must come first as may also be necessary for other children presenting difficult behaviour. Only through systematic observation can staff assess what it is that affects a child's behaviour. Analysis of recorded observations should enable staff to put into place a programme of remediation.

Perhaps every person working with children should here remember the following principles:

IF A CHILD

- If a child lives with criticism he learns to condemn
- If a child lives with ridicule he learns to be shy
- If a child lives with tolerance he learns to be patient
- If a child lives with encouragement he learns to have confidence
- If a child lives with fairness he learns justice
- If a child lives with approval he learns to know himself
- If a child lives with love around him he learns to bring love into the world

Remember:
It is the behaviour we do not like, not the child.

11: VERY DIFFICULT CASES

IN THIS BOOK, we have looked at many aspects of children's behaviour. We have put the debate in context by looking at the national picture; we have discussed why children need an enabling environment and how we can provide one; we have given practical advice on fostering a creative environment and developing a sense of responsibility; we have explained the importance of a behaviour policy and suggested how to introduce and implement one; we have looked at how we can work in partnership with parents and the importance of personal and social development and cultural influences. Additionally, we have looked at specific kinds of behaviour and how to deal with them.

Having read and digested all these points, you may still find you have a child who does not respond to you. With children whose behaviour is persistently difficult and causing real concern, you will need to implement the following action plan:

ACTION PLAN

1 Assign him much closer adult supervision.

2 Give very clear instructions about what he is to do for the next session.

3 Divide the day up into short time spans with clear expectations of what the child is to do – both your choice and his.

4 Give clear explanations of the rules surrounding each activity, for example, 'We don't throw sand.' or ' We don't take tools from other children.'

5 Gently but firmly hold the child's hands and demand eye contact while you speak. Ensure the child has understood what you are saying. Perhaps ask the child to repeat your instructions.

6 Split activity goals into small units – the more difficult the child, the smaller the units need to be.

7 This makes it easier to get an element of achievement. It is through such elements of achievement, no matter how small, that praise can begin. 'Well done' stickers or pendants with the words 'I'm a good boy/girl' are often helpful in changing a child's view of self. Indeed, believing that you're naughty may actually cause you to conform to the label and vice versa.

8 The child is now in the first stages of being 'good' and 'doing the right thing'. You could offer a prize of the child's choice when the child has collected a specified number of rewards. This will give the child something to strive for.

9 Having a collection of 'tokens of acclaim' that can be added to gives the opportunity for public praise at circle time – 'Look everybody, X has been a good boy again and he has another sticker.' In such cases the child enjoys the acclaim and, importantly, other children will begin to change their perception of him.

10 Tokens can, of course, be taken away! But at least you now have some leverage on behaviour.

11 Very gradually, you should be able to relax the rigid timetabling and vigilant overseeing.

12 Gaining co-operation. Co-operation with others is a social skill that very difficult children find hard to master. Under the closest supervision and with the choice of the most suitable partner, increasing time should be spent learning how to co-operate.

Exercises involving co-operation include:

1 Rowing the boat – face-to-face sitting exercise holding hands and bending backwards and forwards as if rowing.

2 Making each other a drink – perhaps lemon or orange squash Encourage the child to ask 'How would you like me to make it for you?' Let the children enjoy the drink and clearing up together

3 Helping a blind-folded partner find locations within the nursery.

4 Playing a simple board game for two people.

OBSERVING AND RECORDING DIFFICULT BEHAVIOUR

If a child's behaviour is causing you concern, you will need to devise an effective programme of support. First you will need to systematically record and date your observations, which can then be shared with parents and staff.

Here is a case study of a child called Janice. She is aged three years and two months. Her key worker has recorded incidents of her aggressive behaviour, and added her comments and plans for action as she follows each incident. Staff in a nursery may wish to use this as a model.

Observation 8 January

Janice arrived in a tearful mood today. When I presented her with the water play bowl and various plastic containers (she usually delights in water play) she did not display her usual enthusiasm. After approximately five minutes during which time she filled the bottles then let the water splash back into the bowl she wanted a cuddle on my lap. 'Cuddle, cuddle,' she said. I asked her if she would like me to read her a story. 'Mme' she replied, which is her way of saying yes. I carried her over to the story box, picked out *Where is Spot?* and began reading to her. Then Thomas (aged three years), who had been playing with the garage set, approached and tried to climb on to my lap, too.

Janice was very resentful and demonstrated this by kicking him away and shouting 'No, no'. When he tried to push past her kicking feet she tried to reach out and scratch his face.

I told her that we all loved her but we did not like it when she hurt other people. 'We must be kind', I said 'and stop trying to hurt poor Thomas.' She carried on half crying and half screaming and it took me about ten minutes to calm her. Finally I managed to distract her with the farm box.

Comment

Janice is clearly very unhappy. Tears have not been far away all day. Her difficulty in sharing with other children continues.

Action plan

Try to raise her self-esteem with plenty of appropriate responsibility and praise. I shall try to foster a nurturing attitude with dolls and toys and comment positively when she seems to care for them. I'll gradually try to include Thomas.

Observation 15 January

I set up a cooking activity. Janice really enjoys cooking and I felt it would be a good way of getting her to play with Thomas. I let them take turns rubbing in the mixture, based strictly on fair timing (I used the sand egg timer). At first Janice seemed to be coping well and I praised her profusely. Trouble began when I asked her to add half the full jug of milk to the mixture. She refused to hand the jug over to Thomas for him to take his turn with pouring. She grabbed the bowl to herself and pulled Thomas' hair. After reminding her that we must all try to be kind to one another and that she must have hurt poor Thomas she said, 'I hate you, I hate you – you bastard'. She threw the entire mixture on the floor and burst into tears.

Comment

We were just beginning to have some success when Janice snapped. I am concerned about her violent action and language. Where is she learning this behaviour from? Why is she so unhappy?

Action plan

I feel I must continue with the praise and play programme described in the action plan above. I will also talk to her parents, though they are not the easiest of people to communicate with, and see if I can glean anything about the situation at home. If things don't improve I'll seek help from the health visitor.

Observation 20 January

Janice was sitting on the carpet with her dolls. She was putting them into bed and covering them up with the blankets I had made specially for the doll play. She made crying noises (for the dolls) and then shouted, 'Shut up, shut up and go to sleep when you're told'. She made more crying noises and shouted the same words again, adding, 'I'm coming upstairs to you'. She took the dolls from the bed roughly by the elbows and shook them violently before taking off her shoe and hitting them on the bottom.

Comment

This violent behaviour enacted against the dolls is very worrying. I feel I will have to speak to someone and seek advice. The outburst of

temper has a dramatic element, with the dolls being punished physically for not going to bed and to sleep as requested.

Action plan

I will do some imaginative play with Janice, involving the dolls. I will model kindness towards them and encourage her to do the same. I will provide her with the necessary resources to play at nurturing and will praise her for any acts of kindness I observe.

I wonder if this violence is a way for her to play out her feelings? – perhaps I should ignore the rough behaviour and just praise the good behaviour.

Observation 28 January

Today I noticed some bruising on Janice. Her left arm has what look like purple X-ray fingers. She has been rather quiet and withdrawn all day while with me.

When her father came to pick her up he asked me if I had had any trouble with her. 'No', I replied, 'Today has been a rather quiet day. But to tell you the truth I am concerned about Janice and the outbursts of temper and aggression which she displays from time to time'. 'She can be a real little bitch at times,' he said. 'She needs to learn that she can't always have her own way.'

I tried to tell him that pre-school children do like to have their own way and do sometimes have difficulty in controlling their feelings. I went on to explain that gradually learning how to behave satisfactorily with other people does develop and it's really a matter of keeping calm and patient and showing by our own behaviour, how it's done.

We both helped Janice to put on her coat, then she suddenly rushed into the toilet and slammed the door. She held on to the door with considerable force and was screaming. Finally, I managed to open the door and remove her hands from it. Her father flushed, grabbed her by the elbow and smacked her so hard on the bottom that she was flung against the basin. 'That will teach you to play around when I've got to go to work,' he said.

Comment

My suspicions have been confirmed. Janice's father treats her very harshly and the violence of his reaction and the severity of the smack were out of all proportion. I shall have to report it.

Action plan

It is essential we provide Janice with a continually calm, supportive and loving environment at the nursery. We must include her in activities in which she will succeed to boost her self-esteem.

BIBLIOGRAPHY

M. Sheridan *Children's Developmental Progress From Birth To Five Years* National Federation for Educational Research (NFER) (1973)

M. Armstrong *Closely Observed Children* Writers & Readers (1980)

Code of Practice On The Identification and Assessment of Special Educational Needs DfEE ISBN 0855 22 444 4

J.W. Docking JW *Control and Discipline In Schools* Harper & Row (1980)

M. Donaldson, R. Grieve, C. Pratt (Eds) *Early Childhood Development and Education* Blackwell (1983)

Mary Hohmann and David P. Weikart *Educating Young Children* High/Scope Educational Research Foundation, Highscope Press Ypsilanti Michigan (1995)

G.M. Blenkin and A.V. Kelly (Eds) *Early Childhood Education: A Developmental Curriculum* Paul Chapman (1987)

Family Policy Studies Centre *Family Change and Future Policy* Joseph Rowntree Trust

Diana McNeish and Dr Helen Roberts *Playing It Safe* Barnardos: tel 0181 550 8822

B. Robson *Pre-School Provision For Children With Special Needs* Cassell (1989)

Dr Rosalind Miles *The Children We Deserve* Harper Collins (1995)

Willstaar Manual (related to speech and language) Willstaar Ltd, PO Box 176 Macclesfield, Cheshire SK10 55W

G. Pugh and E. De'Ath *Working Towards Partnership in the Early Years* National Children's Bureau (1989)

USEFUL CONTACTS

Anti Bullying Campaign (ABC)
101 Borough High Street
London SE1 9QQ
Telephone: 0171 378 1446
Fax: 0171 378 8374

Association for Brain Damaged Children and Young Adults
Clifton House
3 St Pauls Road
Foleshill
Coventry CV6 5DE
Telephone: 01203 665450

Barnardo's
Tanners Lane
Barkingside
Ilford
Essex 1G6 1QG
Telephone: 0181 550 8822
Fax: 0181 551 6870

British Association for the Study and Prevention of Child Abuse and Neglect (BASPCAN)
10 Priory Street
York YO1 1EZ
Telephone: 01904 613605
Fax: 01904 642239

Child Bereavement Trust
1 Millside
Riversdale
Bourne End
Buckinghamshire SL8 5EB
Telephone and fax: 01494 765001

The Child Psychotherapy Trust
Star House
104–108 Grafton Road
London NW5 4BD
Telephone: 0171 284 1355
Fax: 0171 284 2755

Community Practioner's and Health Visitor's Association (HVA)
50 Southwark Street
London SE1 1UN
Telephone: 0171 717 4000
Fax: 0171 717 4030

Department for Education and Employment (DfEE)
Sanctuary Buildings
Great Smith Street
Westminster
London, SW1P 3BT
Telephone: 0171 925 5555
Fax: 0171 925 6971

Hartley-Brewer Parenting
117 Corringham Road
London NW11 7DL
Telephone 0181 458 8404

Forum On Children and Violence
Contact Janet Convery, The National Children's Bureau

High/Scope UK
Copperfield House
190–192 Maple Road
London SE20 8HT
Telephone: 0181 676 0220
Fax: 0181 659 9938

Hyperactive Children's Support Group (HACSG)
71 Whyke Lane
Chichester
West Sussex PO19 2LD
Telephone: 01903 725182

Joseph Rowntree Foundation
The Homestead
40 Water End
York YO3 6LP
Telephone: 01904 629241

National Association For Gifted Children (NAGC)
Elder House
Milton Keynes MK9 1LR
Telephone: 01908 673677
Fax: 01908 673679

National Association for Special Educational Needs (NASEN)
NASEN House
4–5 Amber Business Village
Amber Close, Amington
Tamworth
Staffordshire B77 4RP
Telephone: 01827 311500
Fax: 01827 313005

National Autistic Society (NAS)
393 City Road
London EC1V 1NE
Telephone: 0171 833 2299
Fax: 0171 833 9666

National Children's Bureau, Early Childhood Unit (ECU)
8 Wakely Street
London EC1V 7QE
Telephone: 0171 843 6000
Fax: 0171 278 9512

National Society for the Prevention of Cruelty to Children (NSPCC)
NSPCC National Centre
42 Curtain road
London EC2A 3NH
Telephone: 0171 825 2500
Library enquiries: 0171 825 2706
Fax: 0171 825 2525

Working Group Against Racism in Children's Resources (WGARCR)
Lady Margaret Hall
460 Wandsworth Road
London SW8 3LX
Telephone and fax: 0171 627 4594

Qualifications and Curriculum Authority (QCA) – formerly School Curriculum and Assessment Authority (SCAA)
Newcombe House
45 Nottinghill Gate
London W11 3JB
Telephone: 0171 509 5555

QCA Publications
PO Box 235
Hayes
Middlesex UB3 1HF
Telephone: 0181 867 3299

Parent Groups
Parentline
Endway House
The Endway
Hadleigh
Benfleet
Essex SS7 2AN
Telephone: 01702 554782
Fax: 01702 554911

Parent Network
2 Winchester House
11 Cranmer Road
London SW9 6EJ
Telephone: 0171 735 1214
Fax: 0171 735 4692

Single Parents Action Network (SPAN)
Millpond
Baptist Street
Easton
Bristol BS5 0YW
Telephone: 0117 951 4231
Fax: 0117 935 5208

NOTES

NOTES

NOTES

NOTES

NOTES

NOTES